WITH ARMS OPEN WIDE

POEMS INSPIRED BY FAITH AND LOVE

JAMIE L. CRONIN

WESTBOW
PRESS®
A DIVISION OF THOMAS NELSON
& ZONDERVAN

Scripture taken from the New King James Version®. Copyright © 1982 by Thomas Nelson. Used by permission. All rights reserved.

Scripture taken from the Amplified Bible, Copyright © 1954, 1958, 1962, 1964, 1965, 1987 by The Lockman Foundation. Used with permission.

WestBow Press books may be ordered through booksellers or by contacting:

WestBow Press
A Division of Thomas Nelson & Zondervan
1663 Liberty Drive
Bloomington, IN 47403
www.westbowpress.com
1 (866) 928-1240

ISBN: 978-1-9736-0965-0 (sc)
ISBN: 978-1-9736-0966-7 (hc)
ISBN: 978-1-9736-0964-3 (e)

Library of Congress Control Number: 2017918419

Print information available on the last page.

WestBow Press rev. date: 3/21/2018

Table of Contents

Section 6
Poems about the flesh and its war with the spirit 175

Section 7
Poems With Miscellaneous Themes 203

Introduction

I was in Namibia in October 2007. I had moved to Namibia in January 2006 in response to the Lord telling me, "You should come to Namibia." I ended up staying for 8 years, teaching Bible studies in Windhoek and volunteering at a local church.

On that October day, I remember being sick with a sinus infection and burning with fever. In Namibia there is no central air-conditioning, only window air-conditioners. My window air-conditioner was in the living room. I took my mattress from the bedroom to the living room, so I could sleep under the air-conditioner and try to cool down.

I was laying down on the mattress, kinda tossing and turning, when I saw a creature peaking its nose over the side of the mattress. The fingers of both hands were on top of the mattress, seemingly trying to pull itself onto the mattress. I shrieked, "What is that?" I was scared! Then a voice from behind me said, "Do not fear, it cannot touch you." "Okaaayyyy," I said, still watching this creature trying to pull itself up. "Cast it out," the voice said. Okaaayyyy? I said, "I command you to leave now, in the name of Jesus." And the creature disappeared.

I was burning up with fever, alone in my flat. My head hurt, and I wasn't breathing well. That voice from behind me, a male voice, started talking to me. He told me to get a pen and start writing things down. I knew it was Jesus.

Jesus spoke to me! I asked questions and Jesus answered! Jesus told me never to back down from demons, to cast them out. He told me some things about my past, and some things about my future ministry. He gave me my first poem, which I called "El Elyon—He is Our God." I simply wrote down what I heard Him say, and I have been doing that ever since.

The poems themselves come at any time during the day: morning, afternoon, night, and in the middle of the night. Normally I hear the first line or two, then I hear it a second time, and then I know to start writing. Most of the poems come to me so fast that I can hardly keep up with my pen. A few of them, like "Issues," came over the course of several months. Most of the poems were written straight through, from start to finish, in an hour or two.

One of the most amusing aspects of this experience was that I would hear the voice of the Holy Spirit when I was on the loo, in my flat in Windhoek. I would hear the first line or two of a poem, then I would hear it again. But I didn't take pen and paper to the loo with me! So I would tell the Holy Spirit, "I'm on the loo here!" I would keep repeating those two lines that He gave me until I got the pen and paper. Then I would write them down, and the rest of the poem would come. I called it my "toilet ministry." So many times the Lord spoke to me in that bathroom. Not sure what the location had to do with it!

I like the whimsy of some of the poems, the instructional value of others, and the loving embrace of a Father who loves His children in all of them. God knows what we are going through, and He always has a word to help us. Sometimes that word is a stiff kick in the pants, but all in love! It is comforting to know, a confirmation really, that the word is still relevant and applicable to every area of our lives today.

My favorite part of each of the poems is when the voice of the Holy Spirit kicks in, and takes over from my spirit. Then everything falls into place and makes sense. See if you can pick up the Holy Spirit's voice as you read them. I want everyone to hear the voice of God when they read these poems. And He wants everyone to hear His voice for themselves. He is talking to us all the time!

SECTION 1

Poems about God
And the tremendous love
with which He loves us

"Run to God, His arms are open wide
Your access is through Jesus at His right side"

God's Arms Are Open Wide

"The journey ahead is more exciting than the one behind
Jesus is the starting point, and He'll meet you at the finish line"

Interlude

God's Arms Are Open Wide

Inspiration: Our reaction to sins is very different from God's. We struggle with the wrongdoing, the blame, and the shame. When Jesus took our sins on the cross, He took them all: past, present, and future. If you think about it, when Jesus died on the cross two thousand years ago, and took our sins, our sins hadn't even occurred yet. All sin is forgiven! Enjoy the life Jesus gave us.

> *Scripture:* Romans 6:10 (NKJV) says, "For *the death* that He died, He died to sin once for all; but *the life* that He lives, He lives to God."

There's nothing you can mess up that God can't make right
You are made holy, sanctified by the blood of Christ
When God says something, it stands forever
Circumstances may change, but God will never
Never move from His word, He and His Word are one
When He spoke the words, the thing He said is done
He is not a human that He should lie
He is the same every day, on Him you can rely

If He declared you righteous, it wasn't just for today
No sin you commit will wipe the blood of Jesus away
It is there on the mercy seat, one time for all
The blood of Jesus Christ is more than powerful

It is everlasting, backed up by His word
It is His love, sent to cleanse the earth
Every creation He wants to retrieve
The blood of Jesus cleanses those who believe

A fan blows one direction and then another, God doesn't oscillate
He doesn't move when the situation changes, He doesn't vacillate
That is why it is so important to seek His word first
He can save you a lot of time and give you nothing to reverse
He is the complete changeless God, He cares for you
Once you confessed Jesus, His blood cleansed you
He remits your sins
Believe it or not, He forgets your sins

Before you come to Him
He only sees one sin
The sin of your forefather, Adam
He caused humankind to be condemned
You were born into sin, with the devil as your father
Whatever you did in the past is not the problem
You had no relationship, sin caused separation in the garden
Sin's mark on your spirit is erased by your confession

Rejection of the Holy Spirit is the only thing Jesus cannot tolerate
Even before you're born again, He doesn't retaliate
He made provision for you to confess your sins
Confess and repent, because your sins are forgiven
Child of God, He has seen it all
You are no shock to Him, He knows it all
He knew it before you did it, He told you not to
You heard Him, but did what you wanted to

Sin is disobedience and has its root in pride
If you think you know a better way, you are beguiled
You are more concerned about what your friends will think
When you commit sin, you disrupt the fellowship, but not the link
When you sin, you walk on the enemy's turf
If you hit hard times, it's not because of God's curse
He doesn't curse His children, He only blesses
When He looks at you, He sees you through Jesus

He was spotless and without sin, the perfect sacrifice
Don't lose confidence, come boldly to the throne for advice
You are endued with the righteousness of Jesus at the new birth
With the right to be in God's presence, maybe hesitant at first
You may not know what to do, start talking to Him like a father
Who gave you the greatest, best gift you could ask for
The Holy Spirit dwells inside you and seals you with His mark
It is a spiritual transaction, not a change of human heart

Your heart doesn't change, but your spirit comes alive
God said that with people's spirit He would not forever strive
Righteousness is one thing you never lose
If sin caused you to lose it, this would confuse
You cannot do any works to earn salvation
It is by God's grace through faith, His donation
The average person cannot do anything bad enough to lose it
He is always the same, you become His child when you choose it

Thieves, rapists, and murderers on death row
Child molesters and Enron executives, all of them He knows
He doesn't look to their pasts, but sees in their hearts
Shows no partiality, everyone gets the same start
If works don't get you saved, neither are they your downfall
The sacrificial death and resurrection of Jesus were once for all
He sits forever at God's right hand, He paid the cost
No sin is more powerful than His blood, in it you wash

When you are born again, the Spirit takes up residence
He does not convict God's children, that is your conscience
Telling you to repent, come closer, and seek Him diligently
He blots out the sin, your sins He no longer sees
Trials and tests are gonna come
They are part of the world system
Jump that hurdle, you are strengthened
Ready for the next level, your steps lengthened

God doesn't put you back to the beginning to start again
He pushes you forward, you have gained some wisdom
He doesn't beat you up for your mistakes
No time for that, fear and doubt it generates
Want to hear about some legendary sinners from the past?
Even though they sinned, they were all declared righteous
Noah was a drunkard, he liked his wine too much
Solomon built the temple in Jerusalem, then worshipped other gods

Before Abraham left Ur, he was a pagan who worshipped the moon
David was an adulterer, just looking at a woman he'd swoon
He was a killer who arranged the death of Bathsheba's husband
Moses was also a murderer, he killed an Egyptian
Jonah ran from God, turning his back on 120,000 Ninevites
He had more sympathy in his heart for a plant that died
Aaron, the first earthly high priest, worshipped a golden calf
Somebody who worshipped God was Jehoshaphat

The apostle Paul persecuted Christians
Stoned them, killed them, and did much damage
The apostle Matthew was a tax collector, the most hated of all
But you don't see any of that when you read his gospel
Jesus wasn't originally accepted by His brothers or His family
His mom changed His diapers and wiped His nose, but couldn't see
That He was the Son of God at first, but was there at Pentecost
They turned from their unbelief and counted everything else as lost

Could you do any worse than these have done?
No! When you sin, Jesus is your Advocate
Child of God, do not run away from His guarantee
To Him, you are always credit-worthy
His terms are generous, your debt is already paid
He doesn't remember your sins, He doesn't have an interest rate
He doesn't like sin, but loves you anyway
When Jesus died for you, the ultimate price was paid

His arms are open wide, and His hand is stretched out still
He's always reaching out to bring you closer by His will
If the Spirit was implanted, but then left again
Each and every time His children sinned
That would be confusion, which is not what He's about
Grace is more powerful than any sin, from heaven it pours out
Child of God, do not believe everything you have heard
Go through the Bible to verify everything by His word

If He didn't say it, then don't blame Him for it
He gave you the Book, so you wouldn't remain ignorant
His mercy is something people can't understand
He doesn't seek retribution against His children
He seeks an open heart, willing to follow His path
A yielded vessel, who's willing to serve to the last
Sin makes you feel unworthy, but doesn't change your status
If you sin often enough, your thoughts become distressed

You become distracted and wander away from God's love
Human love is not like His and causes confusion
He never closes the door on His children
Like a drive-through, day and night He is open
He never ignores you, He longs to hear your voice
When you sin, make Jesus your first choice
Run to God, His arms are open wide
Your access is through Jesus, at His right side

Sin isn't all it is cracked up to be
Moves you closer to the devil and further from reality
Further away in your mind, Satan wants you on his terms
Operating in the sense realm with all the twists and turns
Do not be deceived, child of God, sin acts like cancer
It contaminates your mind, spreads, and brings disaster
Death in your mind to the relationship in God's family
But your spirit, once born again, is with God eternally

It is true that He loves without conditions
He loves even the sinner, but only blesses His children
After you confess Jesus Christ as Savior and Lord
The Holy Spirit is planted in your heart, forever stored
Then His love pours out upon you from heaven
His love binds you up, covers you, and strengthens
His love is more powerful than any situation in the earth realm
In Jesus, you are righteous and stand before God as His equal

You are God's child, He could never turn His back on you
He loves you so much that He sent His only Son to die for you
He turned His back on Jesus for three days in the grave
Then God raised Him up by the Spirit, through Jesus you are saved
He doesn't condemn for your mistakes, that is your spirit
People miss the mark sometimes, you are imperfect
Jesus was the only perfect one ever to walk the earth
Accept Him as Lord and Savior to experience the new birth

Love Through and Through

Inspiration: God's love carries us through everything. His love cuts through selfishness and shame and brings peace and joy. His love is unwavering, unconditional, and unfathomable. And I love it!

Scripture: 1 John 3:1 (NKJV) says, "Behold what manner of love the Father has bestowed on us, that we should be called children of God! Therefore the world does not know us, because it did not know Him."

The ride gets bumpy, looking for a soft place to land
Wanting to stand somewhere you know you'll never stand
Get comfy and cozy, window dressing isn't cheap
The price you're willing to pay, whose total is steep

Shame knows no boundaries, its root in pride
Keep looking at the world and figuring it out in your mind
You have the mind of Christ, never forget
He gave it to you, there are some things He expects

Compassion, whose soul is anchored in love
Love that's in your DNA, if you go deep enough
Love that created the world, only to see it destroyed
Love gave you ears, knowing you may never hear His voice

Love that choked on blood and sweat
For those He'd never meet, those not born yet
Love that stands, even though your back is turned
Love through the ages, the deep that churns and churns

Love that never closes the door, only to have it close in His face
Love that yearns jealously as you proceed at your own pace
Never mind the prayers never prayed
Or that you left when He wished you'd stayed

Love that aches and groans, but stands aback
That counted your hairs and supplies every lack
That gave you everything, all the time
Love that says you're always on His mind

God sends you leaders with examples you can follow
Whispers in your ear at night, 'see you tomorrow'
Love is not just a word for Him, it's not just His name
It is His genetic code, the force behind the grace

Grace is power, the Holy Spirit gives it wings
Grace is behind compassion and makes mountains sing
Oh yes, they sing, they dance, they rock the ages for sure
Everything is possible to those who see the way to endure

It's never enough to have everything you want
You think you want it, but don't miss it when it's gone
Keep turning around this way and that
Make about as much sense as a cat in a hat

Recalibrate, reconfigure, and think until you're exhausted
The Lord's way is simple and direct, keep the emotions in check
Light and breezy, His word fills you full of peace
Not the peace of the world, but a peace that doesn't cease

Peace works by His love and comes by His grace
Channels through faith, there's no need to run the race
Samson and Delilah, the sweetness of the honey
You keep looking around and scraping for money

Money is the medium of this time, its allure is a trap
The wallet is never full enough, with or without the strap
The ways of the world are not God's, His are higher
Woven into the fabric from the foundation to the spire

His way is with words, they're filled with love, not hate
You have the choice of when you die, it's not just fate
His love is something you feel, but can't really see
Step off that precipice and don't worry about the next meal

The world will beat you up and leave you to die
Is there anything worse? Certainly God's word is worth a try
Do it because you love Him, even though you don't understand
Hindsight is 20/20, creating humans was God's best command

Seek His face or seek His hand, He offers them both
In time of need you cry out, He's the bridge over that moat
It's love you seek, and He's chasing you with all His might
You don't like the darkness, but maybe you fear the light

You seek something you really don't want
You have to be vulnerable and open to detente
If you hurt when others hurt and feel their pain
Empathize and tear down the walls of shame

It's useful, this resurrection power Jesus gave you
It'll change the world for many, and not just a few
There is power in compassion and grace for the humble
God's love showers down answers, you gotta rumble

Take a tumble, slip and fall, it doesn't matter
His love picks you up beyond the pitter patter
Light as a feather, don't even know it's there
But look behind you, and you'll see Him everywhere

Don't be concerned about the naysayers, doubt is the nemesis
It is so simple, it's the light that projected through the genesis
You seek understanding to keep one step ahead
When you see the next step, don't be surprised if you're dead

Love binds everyone together for the greater good
From Beverly Hills mansions to the recesses of the hood
Malibu is beautiful, its base is sand
Go beyond appearances, or you'll never see His hand

Joy comes in the morning, the new day dawns again
He promised you it would, only on His word can you depend
The swaddling band protects you and makes you unique
He put you on the earth and showed you how to speak

He expects big things, great things that may seem impossible
Love is the human growth factor that makes all things possible
To have and to hold, He knows you so well
You seek a solid toehold, but it's slippery like gel

Don't worry, don't whine, don't grumble or complain
The wilderness is a lonely place, Jesus took all the shame
He keeps the pain from you, He wants to hold it all back
He has to rely on you, so He keeps jerking out the slack

If you love your life, you're gonna lose it, and not just some day
If you lose your life, you live for the Lord's sake
Nuts and bolts, peanuts and toffee, all go together well
His love, His grace, and His word have power over hell

He is never defeated, His chant is victory
Jesus comes again, and when He does, you will see
See that love coming back to get you
Jesus loves you through the end, He loves you through and through

What God Sees

Inspiration: To paraphrase Mark 9:23, all things are possible when you believe. We expand our possibilities by our believing. Conversely, we limit our possibilities by what we believe, or don't believe. If you don't believe healing or miracles are for us today, they won't happen for you. It is our believing that God raised Jesus from the dead that makes resurrection possible for us. For me!

> *Scripture:* John 5:19 (AMP) says, "So Jesus answered them by saying, I assure you, most solemnly I tell you, the Son is able to do nothing of Himself (of His own accord); but He is able to do only what He sees the Father doing, for whatever the Father does is what the Son does in the same way [in His turn]."

Jesus is all that you will ever need
His word is freedom from hunger and greed
From works of the flesh and trying to keep up
He gives you mercy, not shame, boundless love

God's word and His Spirit always agree
Jesus did only those things He could see
He saw His Father doing things, He saw in the Spirit
His mind was human, He had to see and listen

Jesus knew the Law, that the dead had been raised before
More than a carpenter's son, His heart was pure
The spirit of Jesus was perfect before He was filled at the Jordan
His mind was without obstruction, never corrupted by sin

The new commandment Jesus taught was love
It's who He is, His very essence, what He's made of
If you don't know love, you can't know His family
His love is not something you come by naturally

Love is God's nature and burns in your heart
As a seed planted there, just water it to give it a start
People are fickle and focus on what they see
They are driven by what they want and how they feel

God's love doesn't compromise, it's always the same
Shows no partiality and doesn't ask for your name
His love loves those who wrong Him
Who curse His name and speak against Him

He turned the other cheek, so why shouldn't you?
To rid yourself of unforgiveness, it's what you must do
You can't walk in His best if the love isn't there
His church is His family, He counted every hair

He knows where the leaves of the trees fall and tells them when
He brings the rain from heaven and absorbs it back again
You were no accident, He planned your every step
He knows your desires, in fact, He gave you them

When your heart is after His, your heart's on fire
He holds nothing back, every need He provides
Do not worry about tomorrow, about what to eat or wear
Blessings in abundance await, He put them there

Before you know to ask, before you know the need
Above all you can ask or think, exceedingly, abundantly
Child of God, be patient, the vision is for an appointed time
The time draws near, so stay focused, but do not fall behind

Seek God's face, the vision is from Him and with Him
Can't do what you can't see, when your eyes are dimmed
Things of the Spirit are seen spiritually
Walk on the wild side, walk in what He foresees

Press through, break through, and stand in His glory
In His presence is the only way for you to see
You will never do more than you can believe
Build up your heart and get to know Him personally

Pursue after righteousness, it's more precious than gold
It is not a commodity and cannot be bought or sold
It is a status, a condition of being, it is permanent
You have to be equal to Jesus to stand in God's presence

Equal in Spirit, that Spirit in you He provides
You have been recreated, and your nature is divine
Your body is flesh and will always fail you
The word feeds your spirit and is always true

Place yourself in God's hands and give it all over to Him
He shows you what He sees when you are in His presence
He doesn't make mistakes, but often you do
Continue in His word, He is perfecting you

Changing from water to wine, from glory to glory
It is His word that sanctifies, the Spirit who teaches
All things work together for good to those who love God
It all starts with love, love started with His bond

Love by faith and don't corrupt yourself
Faith works through love, love above all else
Get in God's presence, He's in heaven on His throne
Come boldly forward, He will show you what He's always known

Everything God Ever Wanted

Inspiration: When Adam ate of the tree of the knowledge of good and evil in the Garden of Eden, he lost his ability to fellowship with God. We are all descendants of Adam, and are born without the ability to fellowship with God.

But God wants fellowship with each and every human being. His plan involved sending His own Son, Jesus, from heaven to earth, putting all the sin of the world upon Him, then killing Him on a cross. Wait, what? How does that help us?

Jesus overcame Death and Hades through His resurrection from the dead. When we confess Jesus as our personal Lord and Savior, we are brought back into relationship with our Father, God. We fellowship with Him in many ways: praying, reading and studying the Bible, church attendance, singing spiritual songs, etc. This is what God always wanted, fellowship with His children. He really went through a lot to bring us back into relationship with Him.

> *Scripture:* Romans 5:15 (NKJV) says, "But the free gift is not like the offense. For if by the one man's offense many died, much more the grace of God and the gift by the grace of the one Man, Jesus Christ, abounded to many."

The lots have been drawn, the die is cast
You choose your tomorrow, yesterday is past
In the world there is one way to go, that way is down
If you keep spitting in the wind, then failure is your crown

Spiritual death belongs to you, you inherited it
Salvation is through confession, you can never merit it
Salvation is a gift, it's the revocation of a death sentence
There is life beyond the grave, billions of resurrections

The resurrection of life for the good, or death for the evil
No one escapes eternal life, it is the nature of all people
God is eternal, His word doesn't change, He said it's so
He told us everything in the Book, because He wanted us to know

Do not be deceived in the last days, as false prophets come forth
Slice through confusion with His word, the two-edged sword
It all started in the garden, in His presence, God and man
Where humans met God face-to-face, God and Adam

In God's image and likeness, the only thing He kept was the glory
The desire for a family is what started this eternal story
There were trees in the garden for food, and the gold was good
The serpent had access to the garden, which Adam understood

Adam was not deceived or tricked, he took sin upon himself
He was told before that eating that fruit meant spiritual death
Adam fell when he disobeyed, bowing his knee to the devil
It was a shock, but not a surprise, the curse came when he fell

Banned from God's presence, then physical death began to set in
Wonderfully and fearfully made, sickness and disease could begin
Adam was the first tree worshipper, with its lifeless fruit
Eating it was disobedience, in life there really is only one rule

One rule, one power, one authority, there is none greater
No matter what you call it, the blood of Jesus is the consecrator
God's plan is perfect, and Jesus became the key
Adam listened to the devil and became his first draftee

He ate of that tree, knowing full well the havoc it would bring
Jesus was nailed to that same tree, as your sacrificial offering
Jesus came in the flesh, and wasn't just clothed with it
When Jesus left heaven, He had to give up omniscience

Endued with the power of the Spirit at the Jordan River
All the demons started to shake, tremble, and quiver
The power was for a purpose, so that all the sick could be healed
The kingdom of God came to earth, our death sentence repealed

Jesus was the first, but not the only, and not the last
All people should be brought near, that is your task
His kingdom is vast, and His supply never runs out
Eternal abundant life is His promise, so cast away your doubt

Follow Jesus, He is your example, do what He did
Follow His plan and purpose, get filled with the Spirit
Give Him permission to operate through your flesh
Praying in tongues builds you up and gets you refreshed

The Holy Spirit is the life-giver, that resurrection power
Flowing through your veins, yield to Him to get power
Being born again gets you into heaven, that is step one
Being filled with the Spirit means in all things you overcome

Your spirit is born again, and then you have all authority
Your flesh is quickened by the Holy Spirit, transforming to glory
The more you get into God's presence, the more you are filled
It is a constant refreshing, His waters are never stilled

It comes from Jesus, that peace in your heart
We are all family, and His love is the eternal mark
You have a choice to make, Jesus hopes you choose Him
Fellowship through Jesus is everything God ever wanted

Begin Again

Inspiration: When you make a mistake, God is still there for you. Even if you give up on yourself, God never will. There is no sin more powerful than the blood of Jesus. God has more confidence in us than we have in ourselves.

> *Scripture:* 1 Corinthians 1:9 (NKJV) says, "God *is* faithful, by whom you were called into the fellowship of His Son, Jesus Christ our Lord."

Sometimes the truth is hard to face
You think you're winning, but you're just running the race
Lots of snakes running loose in the grass
You don't know, and you can't even ask

God told you to listen to Him, that He's all you need
The world keeps pulling you back down on your knees
You worship God or something else
You worship something, but only He can help

You're on a tether, just swinging around
Loving the height, feet not touching the ground
Wind in your hair, faster and faster you go
Where you'll end up, only God knows

His thoughts are not yours, nor His ways
He counted your hairs and the end of days
You have confessed Jesus, but still follow the flesh
Your life is so confused, it's nothing but a big mess

You ask your friends, but they don't know
They have the Holy Spirit, but it doesn't show
What you follow after becomes your god
He told you about that, but you give them the nod

You're in a cage, and the door is locked
You look surprised, but shouldn't be shocked
It was written on the wall in permanent ink
You keep following the wrong way and didn't think

What would the end be like for someone like you?
God keeps stretching out His hand, but you refuse
The ink is permanent, but not the wall
Years pass by, and eventually walls fall

Nothing permanent here but the word
Everything else came from the dirt
You can depend on the word if it came from Him
It manifests when added to belief and confession

You push and shove and step on your friends
You cajole and lie and deceive and pretend
Manipulate and gossip, it's all witchcraft
Rebellion against God's word, He stands aback

You can stop it all by walking in the Spirit
Put the right elements together, and the fuse is lit
If life seems long here, just wait 'til you go home
Eternal life is promised, life beyond the catacomb

Life is a tender branch, bent by the wind
Sometimes you break, but you are forgiven
When you fall, just pick yourself up
Jesus is here for you, and He doesn't give up

He won't leave you because He needs you
Truth is, He can't function in the earth without you
The mountains move, but only when you say
It is exercising the word that saves the day

Some people don't get it, and some never will
Jesus needs a remnant, only a few fit the bill
If God called you, He won't take it back
Step out in it and prepare for the attack

You won't know when, you won't know where
Only do not fear, the word has already been there
You'll recognize it when you see it
Before that, God expects you to believe it

People pretend and people deceive
People manipulate, always full of intrigue
Only know that God's word is truth
Only know He called you from your youth

Know the word never changes
Know that He teaches you in stages
Step by step, precept upon precept
Wish you could handle more, that you could get it

The snakes are still loose and shaking their rattles
Keep slithering around 'til they lose that last battle
Jesus is here 'til the end, in fact He is the End
Jesus began it all, and He'll begin again

Eternal Now

Inspiration: Everyone is searching for purpose. Some look to philosophy and earthly means. Take time with Jesus to avoid confusion. He's the real deal!

> *Scripture:* James 4: 8 (NKJV) says, "Draw near to God and He will draw near to you. Cleanse *your* hands, *you* sinners; and purify *your* hearts, *you* double-minded."

I gave You everything I had, then Your grace kicked in
When I had no more, Your compassion provided it
You sell yourselves short by not knowing your value
Rush through lives not paying attention to what you do

Taking time with Jesus prevents confusion
Closes out the noise and forces out the intrusion
You are all made the same way, in God's image and likeness
You are inspired life, a human being formed of the dust

You can work on yourself for better or worse
Knowledge of God's word is built verse by verse
Life has a deeper meaning and can't be just about things
Your spirit craves more, and then closer to God he brings

You're drawing nearer to Jesus, where it all began
Your being with Him was always His plan
He doesn't punish His children, He only desires the best
Take on His nature, godliness always profits

It is difficult to discern the way to go sometimes
Peace is established in the heart, leave your thoughts behind
There is a price that most are not willing to pay
The life of Jesus was the ultimate price, He's already paid

God spoke the words and told Jesus the Holy Spirit would come
He would enter into darkness to power the resurrection
To bring that which is dead to everlasting life
To defeat worldly corruption by bursting forth with light

Some say there is no God, they know this is a lie
They all search for truth and the meaning of life
What they search for is purpose
Their reason for existing on the earth

They search and cannot find, their search is in vain
They seek the power God vested in the Lord's name
They want the power but refuse to bow their knee
Just one method the devil uses to deceive

You can have the power, the signs and wonders thrill
But at the end of your days, you will be searching still
To fill the emptiness and to complete that void
Not through earthly methods, forget Sigmund Freud

Philosophy is corrupt, it's created in the natural mind
Can never explain the origins of life
Keep searching the galaxies and exploring outer space
The farther you go, the closer you get to God's face

You cannot now see His face, but only the hind parts
His glory radiates brightly, that is where the beginning starts
It all starts and ends with Him, have no doubt
That first speck of matter, how did that come about?

You have two eyes, not one
Your skin breathes, but provides protection
You are made of water, but it doesn't penetrate
Without the Holy Spirit in you, you cannot truly appreciate

The meaning of life, created in God's image and likeness
Created to reproduce and to overcome the darkness
Not with your power, not with intellect
But with the power of the Holy Spirit as He directs

He calls those things that be not as though they are
Step into God's reality where distance is not far
He lives in the eternal now, where the end is already done
He lives in the spirit realm, it's another dimension

Eternal now means that He never changes
Where all the possibilities are prearranged
When God raised Jesus, time was not reversed
Completion was needed, salvation spoken with words

Grace quickens the dead in the new birth
Your spirit becomes immortal, and flesh returns to the earth
He asks for cooperation, to help Him out and spread the word
There is salvation in Jesus Christ and in none other

His word is truth, and His judgment is just
Redemption is the plan for you, it's complete forgiveness
Take it or leave it, like it or lump it
There is no created being who will ever be above it

The way you choose to live your life
Determines the blessing upon you, that's right
Do you dare to try the living God?
By your words you are justified, by your works you are not

Interlude

Inspiration: This is encouragement to fulfill your God-given task. God had a plan for us in the beginning, and His plan has never changed. Each believer has a role to play. As we keep our eyes fixed on Jesus, we keep moving forward in God's plan.

> *Scripture:* Colossians 1:27 (NKJV) says, "To them God willed to make known what are the riches of the glory of this mystery among the Gentiles: which is Christ in you, the hope of glory."

He called you from the womb for a day such as this
Called you into His kingdom, the one that He established
Built on the foundation of God's word
Built on the Cornerstone, there is none so sure
Grounded, rooted, steadfast, and sturdy
From everlasting to everlasting, can never start too early

The word that bubbles up inside of you is true
From the Holy Spirit through your spirit, a powerful breakthrough
There is none like Jesus, He conveys the eternal plan
Cooperating and yielding, bending your will to make a stand
Stand in the word, even a little doubt can dismay
Proceed in faith and don't let circumstances block your way

Distractions from the world and from the family
Take you off course and steer you away from reality
In beginning the beginning that God began
He started with the word, His vision was vast
Expansive to the end of the ages, He called it forth
Never started anything He didn't finish, never blown off course

As human beings, you are fickle, run this way and that
Try to keep up with the world, believe God when He says you can't
You are no longer of the world, although they would like you to be
Keep dragging you through the mud, it's all they know and see
Days full of busy activities to occupy your time
Not approved or directed by God, they come from outside

He speaks through your spirit, the voice you've heard from birth
You've ignored Him so often, it's almost devoid of worth
You'll come back when you're desperate and got nowhere else to go
Digging down into your inner depths, it's a place you know
You don't visit very often, so the relationship grows cold
God's still reaching out to you, and not just for show

He's in hot pursuit of you, His hand reaching, but you can't see
It was glorious in the garden when you could see
Before sin corrupted you, before you had any cares
You counted the stars and named them when you were there
You climbed the trees in the garden and danced in the meadows
Each day without a care, the animals as your bedfellows

So many generations removed, you can't remember it now
Only echoes of that glory survive in you somehow
You seek the supernatural and the knowledge you once had
Your curiosity is a glimmer, knowing it once existed
A flash of a memory, déjà vu, it is really happening
Because it has already happened, which is kinda baffling

Fear strikes at your mind, asking what it's all about
Then comes the trumpet blast, and Jesus descends with a shout
Re-entering the natural realm, combining the two once again
The way it was when God created it, the way it is in beginning
There is nothing new under the sun
Believe Him when He tells you it's already been done

God calls things to be, you manifest them in the earth realm
Bringing it all back to the beginning, bringing it back to Him
You can't find your way in the dark, there's darkness all around
Searching in the world, what you seek will never be found
God and Jesus are one, and Jesus and you are one
Gathered up under His wings and redeemed into His kingdom

Working the works brings Him glory, that glory He imparts to you
Step-by-step, verse by verse, always closer to the eternal truth
If you don't get the job done, He'll get someone else to go
He has more confidence in you than you know
Not His will, but your will that allows the word to manifest
Jesus is your example, God gives you only the best

The gate is narrow, but the path is alight
Keep stepping forward, walking by faith and not by sight
Walking means forward progress with no stutter step
The past is behind you now but do not forget
Build upon it, because experiences always have value
But don't show the way forward, you must press through

Harvest the wheat, burn the chaff, onward and upward you go
Tap into the Spirit to edify yourself by a continuous flow
The journey ahead is more exciting than the one behind
Jesus is the starting point, and He'll meet you at the finish line
He's already been there and came back to get you
Always reaching His hands out to you, in hot pursuit

The words that He speaks to you, they are spirit and life
In beginning when He began, His glory gave birth to light
The light of His word, the word of the gospel
Good news for ears to hear, for those not grown dull
Work the works, the blessing is in the going
You are His kingdom in the earth realm, start sowing

Light isn't an analogy, but the way it really is
His light shines forth through you from the darkness
Everyone sees it, but some don't recognize
They oooo and ahhhh, and some philosophize
Grab ahold of the reins and move full speed ahead
The rudder turns on your word, all around you is death

Do not be discouraged, you are one cog in the wheel
God needs you to do your part, appetizers come before the meal
The last supper has not yet been, it's not yet time
You haven't eaten with Him yet, but He remembers the last time
In the garden, the trees that were good for food
In beginning when He began, now is just an interlude

El Elyon—He is Our God

Inspiration: My first poem ever. This poem starts with
me writing, and then the Holy Spirit kicks in at "Do His
works and heal the sick." I love it when He does that!

> *Scripture:* Isaiah 48:17 (NKJV) says, "Thus says the LORD, your
> Redeemer, The Holy One of Israel: 'I *am* the LORD your God,
> Who teaches you to profit, Who leads you by the way you
> should go.'"

You know everywhere I have been
You know all the things I have done
You don't condemn me for the things I have done
You only condemn for not accepting Your Son

You give me everything I need
You are the Sower, You sow the seed
Even though I fail sometimes to do Your will
Your hand is stretched out still

You want everyone to hear
All of creation to be brought near
You give us Your Spirit, You give us Your all
You build, You strengthen, and You call

You have given us of Your life
Christ Jesus eternal
You daily forgive our sins and heal our sickness
Cleanse us and purge us of wickedness

To You, the greatest call is to love
Love your neighbor as yourself
Faith, hope, and love, abide these three
But the greatest is love

Do His works and heal the sick
Set the captive free, you have been anointed
You have been appointed
You have been planned from the beginning of time

Not just a thought in God's mind
But the thought conceived and manifested for this time
For this time and for this place
You run this race, you win this race

Time is short, and laborers are few
Each thing He gives you to do
Know that He has placed in You
His ability to do

His ability never fails
His Spirit is all powerful
Do not look with the eyes of your mind, or you will never see
The plans that He has for you, only the eyes of the spirit can see

Don't seek understanding from people
But seek wisdom in God's word
His plan will never fail

You have not because you ask not, or you ask amiss
Do not insist on your timing or your ways
For it will fail in a matter of days

Seek His face
Seek His heart
He has placed His mark upon you
The seal of His Spirit

You are His, declared from the beginning
He will never leave you
He will never fail you
He will always love you

What about you?
Can you say the same thing to Him?
From His plans you flee, afraid to commit
Your heart is not settled, it's not convinced

He already gave His first begotten
Jesus conquered sickness
He followed God's plan
Established from the beginning

Jesus never sinned, even though He was tempted
The life that Satan preempted
Rose again, glorified and magnified
Showed His love, His preeminence, and His permanence

God's intention for you is good
He stands on His word, He is never moved
He watches over His word to perform it
From everlasting to everlasting

He loves you very much, you are His child

He needs you to work the works that He has planned
He only asks, He does not command
You have needs and wants, and all of these He supplies
He will never forsake you, and He will never lie

I do not know how, where, or when, this gives me pause
I know He loves me, because I feel it everyday
I hear His voice, and I feel His hand
Though I know He abides in me, I feel I missed His plan

This journey is a road, a path you cannot now see
Take His hand, and He will guide you
Speak the words He gives you
Do the works as He directs, He will strengthen you

You are never alone

Know that God's word is true, His promises He keeps
He never rests, and He never sleeps
Because He hears the cries of so many afflicted and tormented
Who do not yet know that He gave His first begotten for them

Show me the way, Lord, and I will follow
I seek to do Your will
I will take Your hand, stretched out still

It does not take hours and hours to get into the Holy Spirit
Or to build your heart
It takes commitment and dedication and love
It takes a yearning and a desire burning

He lives, abides, and rests in you
He wants the same of you
Turn your cares over to Him
Cast your burdens on Him
He is here to care for you

When you sorrow, turn to Jesus
When you despair, turn to Jesus
When you question, turn to Jesus
When you delight and enjoy, turn to Jesus

Your sickness is already healed
On that cross, in that field
He left nothing for you to worry about
He will give you many things to shout about

Focus your attention on Jesus
God will see His works in this land for many years to come
Not just a few, but entire nations will turn to Him

They will see what you are beginning to see
That they are without hope without Him
Eternal life, eternally with Him
This is His plan, to transform from glory to glory

Everyone who comes near, everyone longs to hear
That Name above every name
The name of Jesus, His Son, His only Son
Because, you see, He only needed One

He died once for all
Once for all sin and once for all sinners
Once for all time
He is the one who conquered death for all

He was without sin but became sin for you
Not for just one or two
Not just for the Gentile, but also the Jew
He became sin for all

If you can believe
All things are possible for him who believes
Jesus believed, so He spoke
He believed, so He did

He was consumed with doing His Father's will
He said nothing He didn't hear His Father say
Jesus did those works completely unafraid
He knew He would die

Love and compassion propelled Jesus forward
He was anointed with the Spirit
God's life-giving Spirit pushed Him to want to do
And these same things you will do

Don't worry about the vision
Day by day, you will be anointed
When you look behind you
You will see only Jesus

He will lead you
He will guard you
He will keep you
He will love you

El Elyon—He is our God

Glory Cloud

Inspiration: The end is coming soon and we see the signs.
God's desire is that everyone be saved before the end comes.

> *Scripture:* 1 Thessalonians 4:17 (NKJV) says, "Then we who are
> alive *and* remain shall be caught up together with them in the
> clouds to meet the Lord in the air. And thus we shall always be
> with the Lord."

The cloud is already on the horizon
That ushers in the second coming of God's kingdom
A kingdom where flesh is abolished, and all things are new
Where believers worship God in spirit and in truth

The veil of death was ripped in two, torn apart
When the dam bursts, nothing holds back the water
First a tiny spark, then a beam of light came to the earth
His glory radiating and advancing these 2000 years

Light always overcomes darkness, as death has been defeated
The devil's been on the run ever since, his veil has retreated
The cry of the believer and of the church echoes in God's ear
A whisper in the dawn of time, that now is ever so near

The word is so powerful that it can bring itself to pass
God magnified His word above His name, the first to the last
It is true even for those who don't believe
The fiery pit is the end for those who don't receive

In the beginning, Jesus went to the end, it is all finished
He came back to get you, your willpower not diminished
These words He speaks to you, they are spirit and they are life
Powerful and two-edged, cutting back and forth like a knife

The believers are transformed to glory, their eyes opened at last
Face-to-face like in the beginning, the lump back with the mass
You hear about the earthquakes, tsunamis, and storms
You look for God in the wars and rumors of wars

He wasn't in them with Elijah, and He's not there with you
Destruction isn't part of His plan, it's the devil tormenting you
God is the still small voice, the reminder, the conscience
The angel on your shoulder is really there, His promise

You see His handiwork all around, but question its origin
So grandiose are His creations, you cannot imagine
He formed it all with His hands as a work of His faith
Words spoken into existence, hear the crashing of the waves

Perception is reality, that's what philosophers say
The kingdom is just around the corner now, but not today
As the end of this age approaches, the devil steps up the attacks
Diversion is a key part of his plan to get you off track

To take your focus off Jesus, get you to pay attention to things
God's kingdom is not natural, but spiritual, eternal life it brings
Where righteousness reigns, with His face right in front of you
You are sanctified without a spot, not a copy, but the true

Alive forevermore, but still dressed in flesh
Championing God's cause, go forth and gather the rest
Invite them, disciple them, and mentor them
One soul at-a-time, abolish their death sentence

As righteousness increases, so does corruption
Deception increases, mortality whose end is destruction
You control the timing of the second coming, but not its time
Some things He will not reveal, nor will He give you a sign

He warned you of the deceptions and of the anti-Christ
You follow like lost sheep, not looking with spiritual eyes
Focus on Jesus, instead of following the one who leads
Since the beginning God has warned against idolatry

Doomsday will come, but not for those who believe
You lay the sacrifice on the altar, but there is no longer a need
Works of the flesh profit your body in everyday life
Works of the spirit bring you into His marvelous light

On the narrow path, you all walk the Damascus road
Recognize the light or keep kicking against the goads
Rain falls on the tin roof every year, you expect it
There is no life without water, in the beginning God invented it

The manna in the wilderness was no big chore
The water from the rock, each day He produced more
He creates life from the dead by resurrecting lost souls
Transformed to immortal, immortality is the goal

Everlasting life is the outcome, the end justified the means
The world turned upside down when God sowed that Seed
Jesus the Christ is the means justified by the end
Even from everlasting to everlasting, God's first begotten

Jesus was there in the beginning, through Him all things were made
He is there at the end, only through Jesus can the world be saved
Not through your good deeds or your charitable works
Only God judges the hearts, only He knows the intent and purpose

Many are called and few are chosen, but it is not God who chooses
Chosen by the confession of your mouth, the words you use
The cry of believers draws the Holy Spirit like a tractor beam
Pulls Him ever closer to you, He's drawn to the unity

Enoch walked with God and then was not, for God took him
A type and shadow of the rapture, He will keep looking
Searching high and low and sending messengers to the world
Pushing back the kingdom of darkness, the veil being unfurled

Dance the dance of joy and rejoice, for the end is near
The signs are all around, God is making Himself clear
The Holy Spirit fills you with power each time He comes upon you
Power to witness to the world, don't stop with just a few

Get greedy, get hungry, and rev up the power generator inside
The power that raises the dead started with one beam of light
The light is in you and shining through you as an eternal glow
The cloud is on the horizon, and when He calls you, you will know

SECTION 2

Poems about Jesus,
His gift of life,
And what it means
for believers today

"Jesus grabbed control of death from the devil and took the keys
People are no longer subject to sin, unless they just want to be"

Divine Agreement

"Evil corrupts, pollutes, defiles, and drags you down
Eternal life in Jesus makes you a king with a crown"

Credit

"The symbol of the cross reminds you what Jesus gave
But the victory didn't come until the open grave"

Defining Glory

Game Changer

Inspiration: Sometimes we forget about the meaning of salvation. Or maybe we never knew what it meant. We tend to focus on behavior, whether it's good or bad. For God, it is about relationship and fellowship through His Son, Jesus Christ. Once we get those two behaviors down, our other behaviors will change.

> *Scripture:* Romans 6:23 (NKJV) says, "For the wages of sin *is* death, but the gift of God *is* eternal life in Christ Jesus our Lord."

Jesus, the kingdom, what a game changer
He took all the sin, that was the deal breaker
Never again, you are new, refreshed, born again
All the sins wiped away in this heavenly kingdom
Haven't heard of it, this new game?
You'll never be lost again, if you call the Lord's name

Nothing compares, it's the chance to start over
Sins washed away, white like the Cliffs of Dover
You've heard of them, not so far away
They will stand and see the end of days
The end's coming, you know, but not too soon
When all the world hears the gospel comes high noon

Shuffle your feet and twist it around
Mix it up joyfully and dance til dawn
You see it coming, it's all in His word
Imagine living your whole life having never heard
Some have heard, they just don't know
God's talking all the time, He's directing the show

Open up your ears and open up your heart
It's possible for you, it all started at the start
You were created in God's image and can still see
All that is required is to see the possibilities
Who lied to you? Who told you it wasn't true?
Not hearing the Lord's voice is not hearing the truth

The connection is there, established at the new birth
The connection is God's desire, and it moves the earth
God sees you with His eyes, His creation so fair
He hears you with His ears, and tells you how much He cares
To lead and guide you through all the dark places
He loves you so much that He etched it into your faces

You look like God and talk like Jesus, He loves your voice
Billions are talking at once, but He doesn't think of it as noise
Somewhere, somehow, the confusion set in
It's all in His word, which you should be gettin'
You can't hear without it, you can't see without it
The deaf and the blind know nothing about it

Behavior matters, not gonna say it doesn't
But it doesn't start there, it starts at covenant
You confess the word and receive Jesus as Lord
Do it voluntarily, He's not gonna take you by force
Believe in your heart that Jesus was raised from the dead
Resurrection is possible for you, get it through your head

Resurrection happens at the new birth
Righteousness in God's presence, like it was at first
Truth is what everyone seeks, some just don't know
His word has the answers you seek, so give it a go
What you see in the world has your mind messed up
Turn the world upside down by getting yourself confessed up

You gotta play the game, but it's time to change the game
It's not about behavior, but power in the Lord's name
Jesus gave it to you and backed it with heaven's authority
But you backed away from it, and backed away from His reality
You got back in the world's game, tossing balls at the net
Jesus urged you to remember Him, but you went on to forget

You forgot about the change, that new life inside of you
Not a mixed message, Jesus overpowered the death in you
He overcame that force and dropped it to its knees
Jesus inhabits and abides, not by asking pretty please
Death has to go, in fact, it's gone now
All enemies under His feet, Jesus doesn't cow

Be led by the Holy Spirit, and you'll never go astray
Behavior is not the issue, His power is what overcame
Overcame the grave and brought life forevermore
It's a done deal, we're now just adding to the score
Life has issues and difficulties to overcome
You can't do it on your own, you need an intervention

You need power, supernatural and divine
Jesus gave you all He's got, His Spirit and His mind
It's not about behavior, but beholding God's image
Behavior bogs you down, veers you off course, obscures the finish
Don't try to be like Jesus, you only need to follow Him
In order to follow, you need to see the direction

You need to hear the voice of Jesus, you gotta listen
Sheep follow their leader and fulfill their mission
They behave like He does, because their eyes are fixed
Immovable and determined and not getting signals mixed
Mixture is abomination and causes confusion
Confusion is the devil's playground, a deadly intrusion

You stepped off the path, it's ok, just get back on
That's the behavior He's looking for in a companion
When you focus on behavior, then behavior becomes the focus
God told you to focus on the Christ, His name is Jesus
Behavior is about the law, rules, and regulations
His covenant is about love, exchange, and reconciliations

Love is unconditional, seeking your benefit all the time
Exchanging His situation for yours, even His mind
Reconciliation is a ministry, it's bringing you back home
Erasing the enmity, pulling down walls, giving life to dry bones
Eyes that see and ears that hear, spirit over soul
Change the game, shake it up, like rock 'n roll

Way, Truth, and Life

Inspiration: God has a plan for the life of every believer. He gave us His power and authority in the name of Jesus to achieve His plan.

> *Scripture:* John 14:6 (NKJV) says, "Jesus said to him, 'I am the way, the truth, and the life. No one comes to the Father except through Me.'"

Jesus is the way, He gave us back dominion
He is the truth, the reality in the kingdom
He is eternal life, in Him you succeed
He is the resurrection, now begins eternity
You thought life was chance, whatever came to be
Whatever happens, happens, it's all opportunity

God has a plan and a purpose for you
Born of the ages, will you see it through?
The sludgery, the drudgery, and the wondering why
You want the easy road, He wants superfly
Something unique and beyond, a whole new vision
In the world you have strife brewing division

Prune the branches, and the waste falls to the side
Only the strong stand in the wake of the tide
Do not mourn the dead, they had their day
Don't try to go back and pick up what was thrown away
Into the fire, to be cleansed and purified
Salvation in His kingdom is giving life to what died

God's ways are not your ways, we've had this discussion before
The world beats you up, until you can't take anymore
They don't know you like He does, you are His sweet child
You're going the wrong direction, on the path that isn't right
Get back in God's word, it does glorious things
Put it to use how He shows you, in reality it sings

Sweet like a violin, raucous like a fiddle
Melodious and harmonious, rhyming like a riddle
Look back and see what was, the reality that's been
Look to Jesus by your side, He's always workin'
Working together with you, a fine pair you make
A fellowship in love, you've got the world at stake

Day-by-day, piece-by-piece, and step-by-step
Putting the puzzle together, you can count on His best
On the cross, the heel of Jesus bruised the devil's head
More bruising's going on, but know the devil's already defeated
He doesn't have a chance, the deck is stacked against him
The check is already cashed, so he just keeps steppin'

The devil had his day, he chose his way, and he chose to pay
Your ride is free, but there are some words you have to say
I confess, I believe, there is only one way
His name is Jesus, and I give myself today
His love and His life are reckoned to your account
The bill has been paid, doesn't matter the amount

You stand in glory in the presence of the King
All praise, glory, and honor, it's the reason you sing
Climb to the top and look out over the valley below
You were once there, so you recognize the river's flow
Experiences make the person, the refiner's fire is hot
Turn up the temperature a bit to burn away the rot

No callouses on these feet, got no time to get comfortable
Stoke the flames, the time comes, and when it is full
When you have a need, Jesus is by your side and never leaves
The car is gassed up and ready to go, He gave you the keys
The keys to the kingdom are the keys to life
Blessing, honor, and love are some keys to life

Power and authority are the supernatural twins
Take your victories and pile up the wins
You have it all, Jesus gave it to you
Not sitting on it there in heaven, it's yours to use
Power of the Holy Spirit, fire from above
Authority in the name of Jesus, everlasting love

Jesus Was There

Inspiration: Jesus was there in the beginning when human beings were created. He is in every book of the Bible. He gave up sovereignty when He came to earth in the flesh. He went through some things for us. When He was on the cross, at any time, He could have called it off. But He didn't. He overcame sin by His resurrection from the dead. He truly loves us.

Scripture: Acts 2:36 (NKJV) says, "Therefore let all the house of Israel know assuredly that God has made this Jesus, whom you crucified, both Lord and Christ."

Jesus was there at the beginning of time
With His Father, always at His side
He was there at the creation when matter was conceived
He heard the words God spoke, and the things He believed
Where space and time meet
All of creation at God's feet

Jesus formed, shaped, and molded the matter
He made the things God spoke, He put it together
The heavens and the earth were created as one
There was no separation then, spirit and flesh as one
The separation came because of the sin
First Lucifer fell, taking one third of the stars with him

The glory came before the light
The glory radiating from the heavens, what a sight
The glory that clothed Adam encompassed the earth
The garden of God was Eden, the tree of life its center
Eternal life for all was the original intent
Eternal life with God, with everyone living in heaven

Created in God's image to look like Them
Created like They are, in Their likeness
Nothing was withheld except the glory
Deceived by the devil, Adam believed his story
God gave Adam dominion and the power to create
He wanted a family to love, not legions of slaves

The choice was given, and Adam's decision was made
The decision that sent people to an early grave
Eternal life was the intent, but God's hand was stilled
Redemption came through Jesus, God's plan was fulfilled
Jesus was there in the garden when the gate was closed
God separated His child, every day His agony grows

The agony was so great, no cost was too much
Jesus left His heavenly abode to bring you back to His clutch
He risked everything, if Adam could fail so could He
Satan came at Jesus through people he deceived
His disciples left Him in the time of need
Even His family didn't believe

His own covenant people, He led them through the desert
Through the wilderness, between the cloud and the pillar
His commandment of love supersedes the law
God is His Father, Jesus came down from above
People set about to destroy Him by blotting Him out
He finished His earthly ministry in front of their doubt

Jesus was there for every need and to provide for every lack
To show the way and to stand in the gap
He was there in flesh and might and power
With legions of angels, He's a fortress and a strong tower
He was there to raise the dead, the final enemy
Death no longer has control, that spirit bowed its knee

Jesus was there to inspire, encourage, and teach
To show His Father's love and to preach
He was there at the Jordan, anointed by the Spirit
There at Pentecost, baptizing all who were filled
To do the same works and even greater works, to break through
To go forth into the world preaching the gospel, to do

Jesus was there with authority and with compassion
The demons bowed their knees, even leprosy dried up
Jesus was there in the garden, He drank that cup
That cup of sin, He drank it all, to the last drop
Every abomination and malfeasance contrary to His love
Keep you from His presence, thinking you are not good enough

Jesus was bound in hell and surrounded by dogs
He went to hell for the guilty and to empty the synagogues
Those bonds couldn't hold Him, and they can't hold you either
Death and Hades have no power over any believer
If you want something badly enough, just conceive it
Accept any burden, and do what it takes to achieve it

The lashes Jesus bore in His flesh, He felt every one
The disciples fled, they didn't understand His day had come
His mother loved Him and never balked
Her heart broke watching Him carry that cross
He felt the pain, His humanity wanted to shout
He shouldered the cross and shouldered their doubt

Spikes penetrated His flesh, death would bring relief
Then He thought of His Father and separation brought grief
What came next, what no one understood
His life, from the beginning, nobody could
His life with the Father, their connection was lost
Forsaken and left alone, that was the Lord's cost

His omni-present Father turned His back
The devil salivated, demons danced and clapped
Jesus yielded Himself to the devil, that serpent of old
Jesus was in Eden and heard the stories told
The devil couldn't overcome Jesus, because Jesus had no sin
Jesus had to surrender to death and surrender to your sin

Jesus was there in hell, where darkness is so deep
Where the fire isn't quenched, and the worm doesn't sleep
He was there three days, He was there three nights
He was there in torments, but didn't put up a fight
His trial was a mockery, and hell's fire was hot
His Father had forsaken Him, but didn't leave Him to rot

The Lord's body saw no corruption, the penalty paid
God's Spirit raised Him, He overcame death and the grave
Jesus was there at the tomb before the ascension
Firstborn from the dead, He was the first resurrection
Believers get confused and leave Jesus on the cross
He overcame death and paid the penalty, the whole cost

Nation after nation must hear the news
The Messiah has come, salvation is the good news
The truth is that you have it better than Adam, that first man
The Holy Spirit dwells inside you, in your spirit man
More powerful than any sin, His work is eternal
He is imparted grace and blessing, a blasting inferno

Jesus was there when you were tempted, He urged you to overcome
He was there through persecution, He withstood the suggestion
No sin overcomes the Holy Spirit, so you cannot fail
Heaven is yours, just walk in the word to prevail
Your relationship with Jesus is never severed
The bond is unbreakable, you're forever tethered

The victory Jesus gave to you in this life, right now
He gave you His name, to which every knee must bow
There will always be doubters who refuse to receive
Jesus was there after the resurrection for those who believe
Jesus gave you eternal life, with God eternally
Jesus was there, He is here, and will always be

Divine Agreement

Inspiration: This poem is about the contrast between Adam's choice of disobedience in the Garden of Eden and the choice Jesus made to live in obedience, without sin, and to die for humanity.

> *Scripture:* Romans 5:19 (NKJV) says, "For as by one man's disobedience many were made sinners, so also by one Man's obedience many will be made righteous."

It's not like God drew up His plan on the back of a napkin
Even before Adam fell, it was His plan for redemption
Jesus had to do it, because no one else could
Eternal life in the garden, its fruit was very good

Perfect in the day God created him, created nonetheless
There was only light in the world then, no darkness
Formed of the dust, Adam became a living soul
There was no sin in his spirit, he was in full control

Adam could choose death or choose life, both trees were there
He walked in the garden every day, every day they shared
Adam wasn't born of the Holy Spirit, as so may think he was
The Spirit is eternal life, He doesn't turn and run

The Spirit wipes sin away and cleanses every spot
When eternal life is present, sin is not
Sin is first spiritual and then pours over the flesh
Adam accepted sin upon himself and then came spiritual death

He couldn't have accepted sin, if the Holy Spirit was there
Adam had to choose life, so God could bring His power to bear
When you follow someone, you become like them
You yield your authority, when following suggestions

God didn't hold out on Adam, He keeps nothing from you
The word has provision for every need, Jesus gave it to you
Adam ate the fruit and so chose his master
The fall of humankind brought complete disaster

The ground was cursed, and weeds began to grow
From dominion to servitude is a tough row to hoe
From revelation to information, the cord was broken
It wasn't a surprise to God, the path Adam had chosen

God created him with free will and will never take it back
He wants children, not slaves, no yoke around your neck
A yoke steers and drives, removes the matter of choice
When serving the devil your ears work great, but you have no voice

The choice Adam made was once for all
But God's plan was ready before the fall
With sin in the earth, things began to fall apart
God wants you to rely on Him, has your best interest at heart

Jesus came into the world, the first begotten
Born of the Holy Spirit, whose fruit is not rotten
Jesus had no sin, connected to God absolutely
Not born again, but perfect, created flawlessly

Never to die, until after He took on sin
The devil couldn't force anything on Him
Jesus was filled with the Spirit at the Jordan River that day
John the Baptist saw the Lamb of God, who took sin away

Talking about Adam's sin, that corrupted all humankind
Jesus got filled with the Holy Spirit, His ministry perfectly timed
The devil reigned and ruled through people until Jesus arrived
Only by God's grace upon Israel did the Root survive

Wonderful, Counselor, soon coming King
Every knee bows to Jesus, the King of kings
The havoc of lawlessness rules until salvation comes
Salvation guarantees righteousness and resurrections

To be the last Adam, Jesus followed his steps
Jesus ate of the tree of life, only after He was raised from the dead
He ministered as a human in the flesh, but perfect in every way
Sin never corrupted Him, though temptations came every day

In Gethsemane Jesus saw the end and knew what it meant
For the first time, God's Spirit and His would be rent
Angels ministered to Jesus to give Him strength
Then Judas came and kissed Him with the kiss of death

Jesus withstood the trial, though there was no justice
He accepted the stripes, agreeing to fulfill God's purpose
God placed all the sin of the world on Jesus with great joy
The end justified the means, supernatural means God employs

God turned His back on Jesus on the cross, the Spirit left Him too
Jesus yielded His spirit to the devil, to do what the devil would do
The devil didn't put sin on Jesus, Jesus did that Himself
Jesus had no sin in Him, so the devil couldn't compel

Jesus gave His life, even God couldn't take it from Him
After three days in hell, He was raised in the resurrection
Brought to life by the Holy Spirit, the penalty of sin fully paid
Then Jesus ascended to heaven, where He ministers for the saints

Jesus grabbed control of death from the devil and took the keys
People are no longer subject to sin, unless they just want to be
Listen, He was always the Son of God, He did it all for you
Adam didn't have the Holy Spirit, He didn't need to

Jesus ministered to others, He came to show you
To give life abundantly and take burdens from you
To show that the devil is a worm, a defeated foe
That rules as long as you refuse to take control

God created human beings in Their image and likeness
To replenish the earth, to multiply, and to bless
The Spirit of Jesus dwells in you in the New Covenant dispensation
Not for the Old Testament saints, who had not received salvation

Jesus is the last Adam, because He put away sin forever
Get in on the good life, accept Him as Lord and Savior
They agreed in the beginning, so Jesus knew what He had to do
Adam chose death in the garden, Jesus imparts life to you

The devil didn't make Adam do anything he didn't want to do
God put all that sin on Jesus, so that He could fellowship with you
God gave you a better deal than the one Adam got
The Spirit in you means you are always in the presence of God

Creative Power of the Universe

Inspiration: This poem came to me after I heard someone talk about the 'secret power' of the universe. The 'secret power' of the universe is a deception. There is no eternal life in the universe, only in believing in Jesus Christ. Just being a good person doesn't get you into heaven.

> *Scripture:* Hebrews 1:3 (AMP) says, "He is the sole expression of the glory of God [the Light-being, the out-raying or radiance of the divine], and He is the perfect imprint *and* very image of [God's] nature, upholding *and* maintaining *and* guiding *and* propelling the universe by His mighty word of power. When He had *by offering Himself* accomplished *our* cleansing of sins *and* riddance of guilt, He sat down at the right hand of the divine Majesty on high,"

The power of the universe is not a secret
It was created and powered by the Holy Spirit
The universe has no creative power of itself
The words you speak have power to overwhelm
You can speak death to your life, or speak only life
Jesus gave you dominion in the earth realm, do what you like

Understand that if your words and His don't agree
They create confusion and bring death to His reality
It is time to get serious about God and His word
What you create in life is based on what you learn
In the beginning, the world was created by God's words
That same word today upholds heaven and earth

God said 'light be,' and His word went forth
It brought forth light, with the sun as the earth's light source
That word didn't change, the light is still there
For an appointed time, so don't despair
The talk of the world's destruction is just talk
God's word never changes, you can't change His time clock

His timing is perfect, His word is clear
Life goes on until all people have a chance to hear
Hear about Jesus, who brought the redemption
Forgiveness and righteousness are included in salvation
God wants everyone to be given the chance
To hear His word and take a stance

If they've heard His word, they can't say they didn't
Opportunity is given to all to change the life they're living
He doesn't see the way you do: black, white, and colored
He doesn't assign judgment to anything other
Other than accepting Jesus or not
His message to the sinner must be brought

God gives grace to the hearer and seed to the sower
He gives the breath of life, He gives abundance, He gives more
He gives knowledge and wisdom to those who ask
He gives understanding to complete the assigned task
But believers don't ask Him, they don't go to Him first
They seek worldly wisdom and something worse

They give credit to the worldly ways
Satan hasn't created anything in all of his days
The Holy Spirit creates all that is good, but Satan twists it
He turns it into something destructive, it's his subsistence
Mohammed believed in Jesus as a prophet
But there's no salvation in the merely philosophic

There is no forgiveness or salvation in Buddha
They worship many different gods, and that is confusion
In the end, they will bow to Jesus, to that Name
For now they lead people astray, deception is their game
They say to kill for Allah to earn seventy virgins in paradise
Jesus gave Himself to die, becoming our substitutionary sacrifice

You are no good to Him dead, God needs you to live
Spread the gospel, heal the sick, sow seed, and give
He put everything on the earth for you to enjoy
Those false prophets do more than just annoy
They deceive, lie, pervert, and kill
They operate for now, but God's word will be fulfilled

It is God's goodness that brings people to repentance
He didn't create hatred, strife, wars, or prejudice
Poverty is from the devil, and it's not humility
There is not a humble bone in that worm's body
The devil exalted himself to a higher throne
Then was cast out of heaven down to the earth zone

If he knew God's salvation plan, he would have tried to prevent it
So great is God's love for us, the devil didn't understand it
God become a man?
That was the plan?
In his wickedness, the devil could not conceive
Jesus giving Himself to the point of death on a tree

So is everything that comes forth from the Holy Spirit
Satan cannot see it coming, that's how God planned it
The devil can't interfere, he doesn't know before
He is blindsided by God's creative force
It's so important for God's children to seek His plan in prayer
He spells out the perfect plan and opportunity there

Worldly ways are not God's ways and cannot get His job done
When worldly wisdom floods the ear gates, it causes confusion
God's way is to walk by faith and not by what you see
You see only what has been done before, naturally
Step out in faith on the word He places in your heart
His word in your heart is the perfect start

The Holy Spirit will lead you from start to finish
From in front and from behind, angels hedge you in
You are covered in the Lord's blood, so the darts cannot penetrate
When you walk in His will, fiery darts cannot permeate
Attacks will come, but stand firm and show your mettle
Do not let your testimony be stolen by the devil

There are no secrets, the Holy Spirit put it all in the Book
Read the word to get understanding, it's all in His Book
It's not out there in the universe, waiting for you to ask
Confessions are good, but they can become a repetitive task
What do you believe in your heart? That is the key
False prophets and demonic spirits speak what they believe

They use God's methods and truths to deceive
People's words are so powerful once conceived
People can be healed without God or His word, by using gimmicks
Your bodies and minds were made in God's image, without limits
Your mind produces similar results and mimics His ways
But where will you go at the end of your days?

What good is it to live eighty years in success?
Then spend eternity in the pit that is bottomless?
Many do not understand that the lake of fire is their end
Satan's path is the default, if Jesus is not accepted
Grace does not extend to people who are 'good'
If you have refused Jesus, if you all understood

If you refuse Jesus, then God must refuse you
The same process the Old Testament saints went through
Everyone passes through the same gate
Jesus entered Paradise to collect the Old Testament saints
They chose to accept or reject Him, they chose their own destiny
When Jesus entered heaven, His blood covered the mercy seat

There is only one way to heaven ultimately
No matter what the enemy says, his goal is to deceive
There are many 'good' people who will burn in hell
If they do not know Jesus, that myth needs to be dispelled
Dispel all the rumors, the lies, and the suggestions
But God must let people choose, even deception

God's word must go forth, that's why He sent you
To go to the ends of the earth sharing the truth
The universe has no power of its own
His word is the power, in darkness it shone
Everything in the universe was put in motion in those six days
His word has powered the earth's evolution in all of its ways

Satan is jealous and knows people are God's crowning jewel
He damaged the earth once and began his rule
He could not destroy the thing God created
He needs someone's help to do that, so he waited
He deceived Adam in the garden and began to dominate
But God created Lucifer, his every move He anticipates

God did not make Satan, he made himself
He allowed pride to enter and then was expelled
In the garden that day, God's plan was ready
The Seed of salvation was sown, it had to be
When He spoke those words, the process began
It manifested four thousand years later in Bethlehem

God has spoken every word He's gonna speak
His word has enough power to complete
Complete the works He began six thousand years ago
The power generated then is a continuous flow
Because Adam allowed Satan's deception
The seed of discord and death were sown

But it's all coming around in the end
Every sin ever committed has been forgiven
The only condition is accepting Jesus Christ, God's Son
Not the secret of the universe, but the first begotten one
The One who redeemed us from the curse
Jesus is the creative power of the universe

Credit

Inspiration: Believers confess Jesus Christ as our personal Lord and Savior. Our words are the difference between life in the world and life in Christ. When the world tugs on you, remember the power of the word of God to overcome any situation.

> *Scripture:* Jeremiah 32:27 (NKJV) says, "Behold, I *am* the Lord, the God of all flesh. Is there anything too hard for Me?"

You do not give God enough credit
You want to live your life the way you live it
His ways are not your ways, but you don't recognize
Get into the Holy Spirit to light your path, don't philosophize

Your brain is finite, it's brilliant, but limited
God created you to live a different way, walking in the spirit
You fell from grace and fell to a lower level, to the natural
It ties you up and binds you, so you can't live life to the full

Life to the full requires full body engagement
Spirit, soul, and body was the original arrangement
The natural came first and then the spiritual
The two are contrary, a never ending dual

Behind the curtain, the veil that is the Lord's flesh
The veil that fell with Adam's sin, spiritual death
You cannot now handle that realm, the vision too terrible
The destruction was total, the fall devastating, unbearable

You once had dominion and once ruled the earth
But your reflection no longer matches what God birthed
In God's image and likeness, created to rule with Them
Disobedience grew into that tree, from the sin of rebellion

The tree became a cross, the temptation of the fruit overcome
Resurrection from the dead is the victory whose day has come
Your words have power to resurrect, they are the essence of life
The words that change mortal to immortal and darkness to light

The Lord's life was the light of men, illuminating the dark places
He shook the foundations of hell, pedestals fell from their bases
The temporal kingdom is a perversion of love
The devil keeps hammering away, until you've had enough

So will God, He's longsuffering without fail
The devil's got no secrets, Jesus is reading his mail
God created the devil, and in the name of Jesus he bows his knee
He knows God's voice, God's word ends his killing spree

Evil corrupts, pollutes, defiles, and drags you down
Eternal life in Jesus makes you a king with a crown
It is God's goodness that brings repentance, it works every time
Resistance is futile, because God's love stops them on a dime

Don't compare yourself with the world, it will only disappoint
Separation causes anxiety, but complete reunion anoints
Reunion of spirit, soul, and body, as God created you to be
In perfect communication with Him, eternal life in that tree

Between Jesus and You

Inspiration: If you have problems in your life, call on Jesus. He loves you no matter what. He is always reaching out for you.

> *Scripture:* 1 John 4:13 (NKJV) says, "By this we know that we abide in Him, and He in us, because He has given us of His Spirit."

You keep banging your head, there's so much pain
Worldly methods don't work, they only leave you the same
The relief is temporary, no matter what the fix is
The flesh is satisfied, but there's no change in spirit

The angst, the fear, and the lack in every area you feel
The insecurity, the doubt, and the worthlessness are all real
Real in your mind, your father, the devil, is feeding you thoughts
There has to be something better, you feel like you're caught

Round and round you go, trying to figure it out
Your mind is the problem, it controls the doubt
The things you've been told, they're all a lie
Not to confuse you, but it doesn't get better when you die

Life stinks and then you die, you've heard that one
The pit that awaits you is the pit of eternal destruction
Eternal means it goes on forever and ever
Your spirit and soul go there and burn forever

That's right, you were created like God
Spirit, soul, and body, created with dominion
The grave isn't the end for you, you're not like some dog
God created you for fellowship, you are a spoke in the cog

The animals were put here for you to eat, to dominate
The plants are for food and protection and to oxygenate
There are two things over which you exercise no control
God is the first, and your fellow human being is on his own

Everything else was put here for you, you just need the key
The key to life, to love and abundance, your guarantee
His name is Jesus, He secured eternal life for you
Declare Him as Lord and Savior, and then He changes you

The reason for your life, and for living, is in the Lord's hand
He is the end of the world system that destroys man
One or two people will succeed, that is the devil's plan
It's a deception that's bound to fail, the devil is a con man

It wasn't your choice to serve the devil, but how you were born
The hopelessness you feel, your life tattered and torn
You have a reason for living, keep searching and searching
Without Jesus, there's no meaning, seems nothing is working

You seek the supernatural, because there is more than you see
You know in your heart there is more, there has to be
You feel that sixth sense, everybody has one
The voice that tells how to avoid a situation

It's the Holy Spirit calling out to you and bringing you close
He wants no harm to come to you, He wants you engrossed
He wants to dwell inside you and to be part of your every move
To clean up the mess the devil developed inside of you

There is more to life than abuse and scorn
You fear even the family into which you were born
The drugs give you a temporary high and ease the pain
But that spirit inside you is the reason for the shame

You're born of the devil, those are just some of his tricks
Overcome him with blood, the blood that sticks
The blood of Jesus cleanses and protects you
You belong to Jesus, call His name, and He will come to you

You have never gone too far or done anything too bad
God doesn't judge your works or the way you act
This world will tear you up, they don't care about you
Every day there's a new way to take advantage of you

Being a Christian isn't always easy, I'm not gonna lie
But there will be a peace in your heart from this life
You don't have to die to receive a blessing, it's here now
It's waiting for you to receive, just take that vow

Receive Jesus in your heart, He's here now, just receive
Confess with your mouth the thing that you believe
It is the Holy Spirit nudging you, He planted the seed
Not just when you die the death you die physically

The Holy Spirit's your Helper in this lifetime and eternally
You can't shut Him off, He's got no switch like tv
You can shut Him out, by living the way you are
It's your choice, your life, He can only take you so far

He takes you as far as you are willing to go
There's one thing that Jesus wants you to know
He loves you, He gave His life for you, and He will never leave
His arms are open, His door is open, you only have to receive

Your heart is hardened by life, experiences stole from you
You want to receive Jesus, but is He for real? Is the word really true?
Every time you stuck your head up, they slapped you down
How dare you try to save yourself, to get beyond the crowd

God's heart bleeds and aches for you, He wants so much more
You know the way you're living leads to death, you see the score
You can't see His hand, but He's reaching out when you stumble
It's forever stretched out to the sinner, to end the struggle

Redemption is complete and perfect, supplies all your need
Read the Book, it's His word, but most people don't read
The blessings are here, but they don't just fall on your head
Walk in His will, ask what you need, and then watch Him bless

Your life and the way you live is an example for others
Others you know in your situation are still hiding under the covers
Fear rules and dominates their lives, they see no escape
Fear is of your father the devil, he only knows hate

He generates hatred and is a mastermind of doubt
He won't let you succeed, his goal is to take you out
God watches you and cries out for you, His Spirit is hovering still
He mourns and grieves for everyone that is killed

You hear the voice of Jesus, but walk away proud
You cannot do it alone, the devil will take you out
Jesus brought you out of many situations, and you know it
You should have died the first or second time, you know it

It's between Jesus and you, just open your heart to receive
God's Spirit and His Son, Jesus, are yours if you believe
The desperation and fear won't all leave today
You will have challenges, but His light will show the way

The devil will make his grab and try to get you back
Someone dear to you will try to get you off track
You must walk away, shout the name of Jesus, He will rescue you
His promise to you is signed in His blood, He's covering you

That presence at your side is your guardian angel
Mighty and powerful, ministering spirit, he's your angel
He didn't leave you when you grew up, but stays by your side
He's waiting for you to call on him and is forever by your side

Jesus wants to lead you, the devil tries to force you
The devil puts burdens on you and laughs, really he abhors you
It's all love between Jesus and you, just open your heart to receive
God's Spirit and His Son, Jesus, are yours if you believe

Bond

Inspiration: There is a tether between the believer and Christ Jesus. He is present in our lives, not in some faraway place. When you get to a point where you don't know what to do, don't worry. Call on Jesus, He's got your answer.

> *Scripture:* Ephesians 2:13 (NKJV) says, "But now in Christ Jesus you who once were far off have been brought near by the blood of Christ."

Jesus is the Beginning and the End, they are the same
The First and the Last, He has never changed
The plan He gave you is a plan for life
It meets your needs and fulfills your desires

You overcome by the word and through the blood
The life of Jesus bursts forth and covers you like a flood
Henceforth, forevermore, until the very last day
His word is His bond, confess Jesus and be saved

He no longer comes and goes, but is seen or not seen
By the Holy Spirit, the window opens into the heavenlies
The veil has been rent, and the Spirit poured out
Look no longer to the heavens but turn about

In a flash, in a second, in the twinkling of an eye
He is all around you, not waiting in the sweet bye and bye
I AM Jehovah, who sent Immanuel
God is among us, the God behind the veil

Once so far away, never to be seen
Now abiding in you, more than visions and dreams
Alighting the presence and enkindling the flame
All power and authority are given in His name

The light illuminates like a fireplace aglow
They will know Jesus by the power, once you let it flow
His gospel is not only in word, but also in power
By faith it abides, the anointing brings forth the shower

You are the tether by which I hang, the umbilical cord
Feeding me with Your life, increasing me more and more
The bond is never broken, but remains attached
Eternal life in Jesus is a promise unmatched

Golden Key

Inspiration: The Lord's death on the cross meant life for all of us. But the disciples probably didn't understand that at first. Imagine the disciples there when Jesus was taken down from the cross, thinking all was lost. Then His resurrection brought eternal life to all believers. Glory!

> *Scripture:* Galatians 2:20 (NKJV) says, "I have been crucified with Christ; it is no longer I who live, but Christ lives in me; and the *life* which I now live in the flesh I live by faith in the Son of God, who loved me and gave Himself for me."

It's death that causes you to live
Give of yourself, it's all you've got to give
Give it up, give it in, it's gotta go
His name is Jesus Christ, and He's all you need to know

The life that He lived, He lived for you
Unselfish, He died to self, He did it for you
The cross He bore, humility the nail on the left
Shame in His nakedness and the crown on His head

Judas met his Maker, the guilt he couldn't bear
He didn't ask forgiveness, so he couldn't cast his care
The disciples ran from Jesus and denied knowing Him
His end and theirs, they couldn't fathom

It was the greatest miracle ever displayed
A sight they couldn't bear, even to this day
All was lost or so they thought
With the blood of Jesus, the sin of the world came to naught

His death was cheered by many
His resurrection disbelieved
It's never happened before, how could it be?
All things are possible to those who believe

His mother, His disciples, and over 500 witnesses testified
They saw Jesus walking, talking, and eating after He was glorified
He walked through walls, wouldn't you love to do that?
Ate fish with His disciples, had a fireside chat

The fruit Adam plucked from the tree
The weight of the world that once fell on his body
Every sin that you know or that will ever be
Entered the world through the fruit on that tree

Adam couldn't handle it, he was just flesh
Without the Holy Spirit, there is no progress
With the Holy Spirit, you can do all things and see all things
His knowledge is far-reaching, His life is everlasting

God's word never changes, though you sometimes do
The Lord's resurrection was once for all, and for you too
For the unborn, both old and young
The sinner, the unworthy, and all who will come

Jesus bore the temptation, He bore the shame
Forget about the deception, but remember His name
It's a golden key, purified by fire
He rescued everyone with the nail on the right

The weight of the world that only Jesus could bear
The disciples watched Him die in the depths of despair
Every nerve, every tissue, every bone, and sinew
Contaminated with sin, so that it never touches you

Disobedience makes you wanna run and hide
Comes from arrogance and plain old human pride
Sickness and disease were borne in His stripes
In the nail in His feet and the slash in His side

Receive the name of Jesus and receive His glory
His death was only the beginning of the story
It ends with you, in a nick of time
He was raised from the dead and then elevated to the sky

There is nothing new under the sun, Jesus went before you
He took all the sin and became the fruit
He went first, so you can follow Him faithfully
He became the Last, so that you would have the Key

Defining Glory

Inspiration: This poem is about the birth, life, death, resurrection, and ascension of Jesus Christ. We all have crosses in our houses, as necklaces, etc., to commemorate that Jesus died for all sinners. But His victory over death didn't come until the open grave. The resurrection of Jesus from the dead is what gives us eternal life. Jesus is the only person ever resurrected from the dead, never to die again. It is His resurrection life that flows through our veins, as believers. Jesus is alive, and He lives in us! Glory be to God!

Scripture: Romans 8:11 (NKJV) says, "But if the Spirit of Him who raised Jesus from the dead dwells in you, He who raised Christ from the dead will also give life to your mortal bodies through His Spirit who dwells in you."

He was born of the Holy Spirit, the Seed incorruptible
He was born again the same way, His glory indestructible
The death that He died, He died for you
There is no limit to what God's love will do for you
Born of the Holy Spirit to Mary of Nazareth
Jesus came into the world as a man, in the flesh

There was no other way for people to be redeemed
He was King of kings, but not esteemed
People look to His cross and see His body broken
The crown of thorns and the shame of the moment
It was the sin of the world that crucified Him
Once for all, every sin was transferred to Him

But listen, Jesus was born to do it, there was no other way
When Adam ate the fruit of the tree, there was a price to pay
Adam's spirit was pure, but died after the sin
God covered Adam's transgression with animal skins
God's creation was lost and subjected completely
To sin and sickness, to death and disease

Dominion shifted from Adam to Satan
That old deceiver danced and celebrated
God's greatest creation fell into his hands
The destruction encompassed even the land
But God created Lucifer, and his every move is anticipated
Lifted up by pride, he fell from the sky, his power overrated

God's word went forth immediately after Adam's fall
The Seed of the woman sent to save us all
The prophets wrote about Jesus, even Moses knew
The law was temporary, it couldn't do what God needed it to do
The law covered the sins, but never removed the sin
God mourned as He watched His servants blind and struggling

His Son, Jesus, arrived at the appointed time
He went to the Jordan River to be baptized
Empowered by the Holy Spirit, He began to minister
Showing us the possibilities, as He walked the earth
To do and teach, to demonstrate His power
Jesus ushered in the era of grace, this final hour

He was tempted by Satan, but overcame
Jesus walked in the flesh, on His knees He prayed
He was limited by His flesh, but overcame in the Spirit
In God's Spirit there is power, perfect strength without limit
Jesus cast the devil out and started taking back control
To teach people the way, it wasn't just some show

God endued Jesus with power, His life was eternal
Jesus had to give up the Holy Spirit, so you could be immortal
The agony in Gethsemane was not physical
Jesus faced separation from His Father, the pain was spiritual
He was with God in the beginning, He formed the earth
He created it through the Spirit, who brooded and hovered

There in the beginning: Father, Spirit, and Son
They had never experienced separation
Jesus was on the earth before, in the cloud and the pillar
A temporary assignment for forty years in the desert
This earthly assignment could be His last
He spent forty days in the wilderness to fast

One stumble, one lie, and He would be disqualified
There could be no sin in Him in order to impart eternal life
He was a man, tempted in every way as are you
Women, alcohol, and money tempted Him too
He overcame, because He saw the end from the beginning
Before God sent Him out, He imparted the vision to Him

Jesus became poor, so that you might become rich
He put His inheritance on the line, it was a risk
The love in His heart was built up in prayer
His plans and purposes were defined there
God spoke to Jesus the same way He speaks to you
By His Spirit, He guided Jesus through the works He would do

When Jesus went to the cross, His flesh cried out
Beaten, tormented, and forsaken by their doubt
But He drank the cup God gave Him, whatever He had to do
It wasn't about pain and suffering, it was about you
For three days in hell, the devil surrounded Him
Jesus gave His life, Satan tortured and pounded Him

Although your body dies, your spirit lives forever
In hell tortured and burned, but alive forever
The deception, the accusations, and all the sins of the world
Upon Jesus, in three days and nights, all that sin was hurled
The Holy Spirit descended and imparted His glory
Jesus was made alive and then raised up for all to see

Imagine the devil's surprise, his week that started in victory
Ended in total disaster for his kingdom, in eternal defeat
The power of the Holy Spirit is the power of the resurrection
First to be raised in glory was Jesus Christ, God's Son
The angels danced when the rock was removed from the tomb
Jesus defeated the enemy and sealed his doom

His flesh glorified, Jesus ascended to heaven
Seated at God's right hand, forever ministering
In Paradise, the Old Testament saints were released
Everyone gets to heaven the same way, by bowing their knees
Jesus returned to earth to announce the good news
His birth was a big deal, His resurrection couldn't be refused

Many saw Jesus alive, hundreds were His witness
Jesus imparted the Holy Spirit to the believers at Pentecost
Celebrate His birth and rejoice in His resurrection
It is the power of the Spirit that brings salvation
You are saved by the Spirit, with your mouth you confess
You saw the healings and miracles while Jesus lived in the flesh

You have that same power residing in you
Anointed to do the works God gives you to do
His anointing is for action, once you step out
Don't sit there waiting for it, His grace pours out
Answer His call, get up and do
There is so little time, you must pursue

Do not look to the cross, considering it a loss
The sacrifice was the Lord's flesh, His life was the cost
Flesh gets you nowhere in God's kingdom, you'll find
Salvation is a spiritual thing, your nature becomes divine
The symbol of the cross reminds you what Jesus gave
But the victory didn't come until the open grave

Don't think with your mind, just follow your heart
The end is near, so God needs you to do your part
Jesus left the earth and gave you all authority in His name
Go out and do the works, your authority is the same
His Spirit dwells in you, you are God's eternally
His Spirit is transforming you from glory to glory

You have the power to raise people from the dead
By the words of your mouth, God's plan moves ahead
Maybe you don't get it, your sins are forgiven
The sins of everyone on earth have been remitted
Make a confession of your mouth to receive
Salvation is available for everyone who believes

All your past sins are forgiven
All your future sins are forgiven
The sins of those yet sinners are forgiven
Jesus bore all sin, for all time, for all men
Walk in the glory, He earned it for you
Spend time in God's word to learn it through and through

His passion is for the sinner, He loves them all
Jesus cleanses all unrighteousness when they answer His call
God is omnipotent, but steps aside and allows you to choose
Jesus fulfilled His purpose in giving His body and blood for you
Do not look to His cross as the end of the story
Look to the resurrection of Jesus, it is His defining glory

Until Jesus Comes

Inspiration: During the communion service, we remember that Jesus died for our sin. He had no sin of His own. He paid the penalty, so that we don't have to! His death removed the curse of the Old Testament. The New Covenant is His blood.

> *Scripture:* 1 Corinthians 11:24-25 (NKJV) say, "and when He had given thanks, He broke *it* and said, 'Take, eat; this is My body which is broken for you; do this in remembrance of Me.' In the same manner *He* also *took* the cup after supper, saying, 'This cup is the new covenant in My blood. This do, as often as you drink *it*, in remembrance of Me.'"

God's word is true, the covenant has been established
Jesus died once for all, did you get the message?
But how can they hear, unless someone is sent?
Preach the word, it is forgiveness and redemption
God's covenant is everlasting, His word never fails
The blood of Jesus covers the mercy seat, He tore the veil

His blood paid the price, which was well worth the cost
One win in the victory column, the devil bore the loss
Jesus satisfied every claim ever made
He holds the title deed, even to this day
Not with the blood of goats and lambs
But with His own blood, His life in His own hands

He could have turned His back, no one would blame Him
Die for sinners? Gentiles? Who else would claim them?
Jesus sacrificed His flesh and poured out His blood
The price paid for every sin, its power unplugged
Once your spirit is cleansed, you are God's forever
As often as you take communion, you remember

The Lord's life and His death, He did it all for you
He never looks back, He knew what He had to do
Jesus is coming again, that is His promise
To raise you up and clothe you in eternal garments
The Holy Spirit flows like a river and dwells inside you
Changed you from death to life, you are born anew

The Old Testament is abolished, there's no longer a need
The New Testament is the blood of Jesus, signed and sealed
There can be no covenant unless blood is shed
A covenant cannot be cancelled, except by death
You must choose this day whom you will serve
God's ways are not the ways of the world

Come out from among them and keep yourself clean
Follow through on God's commands and be willing to yield
They entice you, distract you, and lead you bit-by-bit
They don't pull you away all at once with one hit
Today is planted doubt, tomorrow is fear
You must choose whose voice you will hear

Child of God, His precious shining jewel
He put you on earth to have dominion, to rule
Get out front and lead like the Pied Piper
Not just sit around and play church, remove the diaper
You should be ready for meat, but cry out for milk
Lead others to salvation once your belly is filled

Look at Jesus, who endured the cross set before Him
Because of the joy that would come after Him
Hosanna in the highest! Peace and goodwill to all!
Peace comes after the battle, to those who answer the call
Of course, Jesus will never die
Sitting forever at God's right side

When you remember the death of Jesus, focus on His life
Eternally ministering for you, His flesh glorified
Jesus redeemed you from the curse and blessed you mightily
The blessing of Abraham through Jacob and Isaac
You are endued with righteousness, a gift of His grace
Go boldly forward and speak to Him face-to-face

God doesn't see your sins, tell Him once and forget 'em
Jesus paid the penalty in full, so He remits 'em
He is the bread of life, and His word nourishes you
Come together for communion, and as often as you do
You remember the death of Jesus, His life and His love
This do in remembrance of Jesus, until He comes

SECTION 3

Poems about the gift of the Holy Spirit And the gifts He imparts to us

"If there is no light in you, you are blind
Without God's Spirit to guide you, you are led by your mind"

Eye of the Body of Christ

"The Holy Spirit will change and renew
He cannot enter without making a new you"

God's Spirit in You

The Eye of the Body of Christ

Inspiration: The Holy Spirit dwells in every believer. He empowers us, leads us, and counsels us. He confirms God's word in our lives. He is the eye of the body of Christ.

Scripture: 1 Corinthians 2:9-11 (NKJV) say, "But as it is written: *'Eye has not seen, nor ear heard, Nor have entered into the heart of man The things which God has prepared for those who love Him.'* But God has revealed *them* to us through His Spirit. For the Spirit searches all things, yes, the deep things of God. For what man knows the things of a man except the spirit of the man which is in him? Even so no one knows the things of God except the Spirit of God."

The Holy Spirit is the eye of Christ's body on earth
It is He who sees where to work the works
The gifts of the Spirit operate as He wills
He dwells in every believer, when you ask Jesus, He fills
The Spirit comes upon you with His power and personality
He is here in the earth realm now, only ask to receive

If there is no light in you, you are blind
Without God's Spirit to guide you, you are led by your mind
You are fearfully and wonderfully made, it's true
The mind does nothing compared to what the Holy Spirit can do
Can you walk on water without any faith?
Can you cast anything out without authority in the Lord's name?

Can you move kingdoms and dispel darkness?
The minds of human beings created this earthly mess
Keep building and building and use up the fossil fuels
The earth's system is failing, you already see the clues
Let the Holy Spirit guide you, and He will show you the way
He has the answer even in this late day

He is the light that shines in the darkness
Without the Spirit, everything in life is just a guess
You cannot know God's Spirit without knowing His word
He cannot dwell inside you until you experience the new birth
Why does God's creation want to walk around in the dark?
He created you like Him: spirit, soul, and body; tri-part

You feed your body and titillate your mind
Your spirit groans with birth pangs on the inside
The feud goes on in the flesh, warring against your spirit
Until your mind is renewed in the word, by your flesh you are led
God did not create you like the animals
To be led by your needs or what is tangible

When you are led by your flesh, the devil delights
This is his territory, his demons work in you to excite
They excite anger, greed, envy, and all sorts of emotions
Anything they can do to keep you away from Jesus
The spirit of a human being is the candle God uses
To light the dark places, with light they are infused

No one lights a lamp and puts it under the table
They put the light on the table and so enable
Enable everyone in the room to be blessed by the light
Everyone sees God's Spirit in you, if you walk right
That light under the table is the seed of salvation
Being filled with His Spirit brings full illumination

God's Spirit upon you infuses the world
With His power and His word enveloping the earth
The speed of light is faster than anything we know
Turn on the switch, and in an instant the room is aglow
So it is with His Spirit, the power is there
It is the power of salvation to those in despair

The eye is the radar of the body, its guidance system
People follow what their eye focuses on with little resistance
But not so for God's child, His Spirit leads
When the light is under the table, His Spirit grieves
Because there is so much more He wants to do for you
But how can He? Unless He can channel power through you

God needs vessels who are willing to follow the commands
If you hear Him, but do not do, nothing prospers in your hand
If you walk in the natural, the instructions seem impossible
Do you believe His word? With Jesus all things are possible
Possible to him who believes, it's time to change your thinking
Line up with the word, new wine you are drinking

Build yourself up in God's word by meditating
By praying, by giving Him first place, and by relating
Relate everything in your life with Him, keep a dialogue
Pray in tongues, but prayer should not be a monologue
Stay quiet and listen for God's voice
He will speak to you and show you the right choice

A believer's life shouldn't be up's and down's
Always guessing and trying to figure things out
Jesus told you His yoke is easy, and His burden is light
When He enters the battle, it is not to fight
But to strengthen you in faith, the victory's already won
You are more than a conqueror, the battle is already done

By Jesus, that day on the cross, He bore your sin and sickness
He defeated the devil after three days' separation in darkness
The agony Jesus felt in the Garden of Gethsemane
Had nothing to do with pain, or humiliation, or human frailty
He was always with His Father since the beginning of time
He was one Spirit with God, His nature is divine

They had never parted, had never been separated
That's why Satan for three days danced and celebrated
He thought he had conquered Jesus
Satan thought he ruled over his nemesis
The separation of Jesus in hell is what every sinner feels
Alienation, frustration, and hopelessness that seem real

God's Spirit always led Jesus until He died in the flesh
Only without the Spirit could Jesus experience death
God's Spirit is His power unleashed in the earth
In every believer it is given to discern
His voice allows you to operate in the supernatural
Led by that voice in your mind, you keep hitting a wall

God's Spirit calls each one to minister what you believe
Not everyone needs to preach, that's not necessary
You'll win believers by the way you live
By the peace in your heart, and the love you give
God's Spirit is His fullness, in Him all ability rests
You limit yourself running the race with no endurance

The Holy Spirit renews, strengthens, empowers, and builds
He guides, counsels, and shows how dreams are fulfilled
He gives hope to the hopeless
Floods light into the darkness
He heals the sick and rights every wrong
He inspires, encourages, and powers the resurrection

It is said computers store the knowledge of the earth
That is nothing compared to the miracle of the new birth
Mortal is changed to immortal in an instant
That sown in corruption becomes incorruption
This is not some new phenomenon or some magic act
It is the power of the Holy Spirit to resurrect

It is a spiritual principle, not a natural law
By a declaration of Jesus as Lord, you become immortal
Become as He is, immortal in heaven
Lord and Savior, He's our confession
He gives of His Spirit, you become a part of His family
Forever led by the Holy Spirit, the eye of Christ's body

Sowing Seed

Inspiration: We sow seed financially, by the words that we speak, and the deeds that we do. The Holy Spirit plants the fruit of the spirit in our spirit, enabling us to sow into the lives of others. Believers show others what God is really like.

> *Scripture:* Gal 5:22-23 (NKJV) say, "But the fruit of the spirit is love, joy, peace, longsuffering, kindness, goodness, faithfulness, gentleness, self-control. Against such there is no law."

God's kingdom has a system that is not of the world
Created before time, before there was a world
He created it with seed time and harvest
The seed must first die, then life arises from the carcass

The sower doesn't always reap, it is left to others
Generation after generation, the field is white for harvest
God sends you to the field, not to pluck and eat
But to train them up in the way they should go, like babies

You cannot hear without listening to what is said
The gospel is spoken, and the Holy Spirit gives the go ahead
It is a simple word, complete freedom
Move on it when you hear and remove the burdens

God's kingdom operates through faith, sustained by grace
He knows you have need of things before you pray
Your word is the seed, with it you create
For better or worse, its power you must appreciate

A seed of doubt subdues God's people
Fear immobilizes, its motive only evil
Fear is a burden that causes you to stutter
Has physical effects which turn your rudder

Stress causes you to draw your next breath
Fear causes hesitation then draws you to darkness
Don't draw back from it, but cast it out in the Lord's name
The seed once planted grows, this is not a game

Sickness isn't from God, but has its root in the garden
The seed was planted in your heart, planted within
Use your words to pluck it out, the power is there
Over time roots grow deeply and crack the foundation layer

Words change your heart when heard over and over again
Faith comes by hearing the word of God, and hearing
Be careful what you hear and be careful how you hear
Light repels darkness, let His word be clear

The fruit of the spirit is planted in your heart at salvation
Righteousness means a clean slate, freedom from damnation
Enter God's presence without fear or condemnation
Through Jesus Christ all sin is forgiven, complete sanctification

He loves even the sinners, He forgave them once for all
By your free will, you choose to rise or fall
There is power in liberty and power in love
Not like power of the world that brings destruction

Founded by the devil, its failure guaranteed
The system's root is pride, pride is the seed
Grab everything you can get without care for neighbors
The foundation is bad, its roots rotted to the core

God's joy is your strength, it's rooted in love
Mercy and compassion, whose limits are boundless
Seeds are planted every time a word leaves your mouth
People watch your lifestyle to see what God is about

You represent Jesus as priests and ambassadors
You are in charge, so be bold in recognizing your source
Peace rules in your heart, judging like an umpire
The New Covenant is patience, not a consuming fire

Patience is a long-term strategy and not just for today
God longs for His creation to come near, for everyone to be saved
He forgives your sins and remembers them no more
The choice He made to fellowship, to never close the door

People do stupid things, they stumble, and some fall
God's heart forgives and forgets, His love is eternal
He chose you from the beginning to be like Him eternally
The life you live, every deed, is a reflection of His glory

Love does good to a neighbor and does him no harm
Does not retaliate, but embraces him with open arms
Kindness to a stranger is kindness on God's behalf
Gives you His identification, taking a step on His path

Applying God's word in your life gets the job done
Hearing comes by faith, His word brings salvation
Angels can't get people saved, they minister to the saints
Faith comes by hearing, and God's word never changes

Goodness is a heart after Jesus, it is your character
When no one is watching, are you practicing His word?
More than playing church or keeping up appearances
God's word is the strong foundation, test the spirits

You are His reflection, only He is good
Forces of doubt and unbelief must be withstood
Meekness is peace in your heart, that inner glow
Outer adornments are nice, from inside God's Spirit shows

A reflection of Jesus in youth and vitality
He adds years to your life when you walk in humility
It is not poverty, you don't have to walk in lack
The devil stole from you, speak God's word and get it back

Tithers are protected, the devourer He rebukes
Be careful where you step, stay away from disputes
Temperance is self-control, it's a matter of your will
Jesus is the same every day as an act of His will

He is God, He knows it all, and can do what He wants
But He will not violate His word, He made that decision
If He changed every day, what would you do?
He is Jehovah Raphe, the God who healed you

Who guides you, protects you, and leads you by waters still
He raised you to His right hand with Jesus, His promises fulfilled
You can rely on Him and His covenant, He will not break it
He's El Shaddai, if the thing doesn't already exist, He creates it

God answers your prayers, because He said He would
For sure, forever, and for always, His word is good
His word is His seed, planted inside you
He fulfills His word, and He expects the same of you

Seed time and harvest, He said they will never cease
Rest in His word, there is nothing like His peace
Faithfulness is rewarded in every area of your life
Doing His word is the application, rightly divided

His seed is planted in you, by the Spirit you bring it out
His presence waters and fertilizes the ground
The seed you control, and your confession rules the harvest
A negative confession is how the Spirit is quenched

The timing of the answer is the thing only He knows
His timing is perfect, the Lord of the harvest overflows
The seed, the ground, and the exact moment in time
Tares are weeds like discord and strife

Works of the flesh are designed to destroy, kill, and steal
Like a boll weevil gnawing at the root, the damage is real
Religion is a seed whose purpose is to mislead
Follows rules and regulations and doesn't think spiritually

An abomination, a stench, white tombs with dead man's bones
Jesus preached division, him with no sin throws the first stone
God's grace is power, if you can understand it
Shows no partiality, that's how He planned it

There's power in forgiveness, not in accusation
Tradition obscures truth with a slight modification
Eases your conscience, but doesn't change the heart
Can never conquer the flesh, strongholds get head-starts

Seeds start revolution and when planted in good ground
They produce a harvest that changes the world all around
The seed fights to break through the soil
Is vulnerable at every stage and requires consistent toil

Seed produces a harvest that reproduces fruit
Generations of harvest come when using proper tools
Produce a harvest with the fruit that comes spiritually
In the beginning, it all started with God's word and Seed

Refreshing

Inspiration: The refreshing of the Holy Spirit comes by spending time in the word, through singing hymns, psalms, and spiritual songs, by praying in tongues, and by fellowshipping with the Holy Spirit, among other things. Refreshing strengthens believers.

Scripture: Acts 3:19 (NKJV) says, "Repent therefore and be converted, that your sins may be blotted out, so that times of refreshing may come from the presence of the Lord,"

This is the time of the refreshing
Come closer to God and receive His blessing
You have been anointed from the new birth
The Holy Spirit comes upon you, quenching your thirst
Take a drink, drink deeply, and lose your breath
God's Spirit upon you is the rest with which you rest

You are taken from the ordinary and completely refreshed
When His power comes upon you, every lack is quenched
God's Spirit is a consuming fire, who lights up dark places
He purges excesses and fills up empty spaces
He imparts the fruit of the spirit, and then builds them into you
Compels you to exercise them, as He's working through you

Ask to receive the Holy Spirit, He is who you receive
He is available through Jesus Christ to everyone who believes
Don't be drunk with wine, but filled with God's Spirit
It is not a one-time transaction, as in 'fill up and forget it'
Each time you seek God's face and seek Him from your heart
His Spirit fills you up again, praying in tongues is just one part

Sing hymns, psalms, worship, and praise
Get into the Holy Spirit, there are so many ways
Service is worship, by which you are strengthened
A continuous flow of His Spirit proves the redemption
Do not look left, do not look right, but focus specifically
Tongues is not the only way to grow spiritually

God's anointing is the power that breaks yokes
His power is not just in baby steps, but in master strokes
He gives you as much as you are willing to receive
It's a heart issue, and He gives you more as you yield
Not to store up and use just for you and your needs
Look beyond yourself, there is a whole world to feed

So many have not heard God's word, they are lost
They won't come to your palace, if they can't afford the cost
Get out there and bring them in, they knock on your door
The clock keeps ticking, He is keeping score
They are knocking on your door in the spirit realm
Can you hear them? Or are you too caught up in yourself?

God's anointing is for souls, so win them any way you can
Heal them, deliver them, and set them free, it's the master plan
His anointing is not just for you and your stuff
What did He mean when He said you left your first love?
Your first love was Jesus, remember the day you got saved?
Your heart was filled with joy, and peace rolled in like a wave

You jumped and shouted and danced with glee
Then focused on earthly treasures and forgot about reality
It's ok, there's still time to turn yourself around
You can't do it all by yourself, teaching must be sound
Soul winning is God's passion, there is so little time
His anointing is upon you, prosperity is simply a sign

Prosperity is the means, not the end, to spread His gospel
It is not gospel when you focus on things more than souls
People must be taught the right way to go
The fruit produced in their lives is how you will know
God's word says to train the child up, we all start as children
Bring them in, teach them the word, and establish them

Correct the bad teaching to get them on the right track
Their exuberance will bring others to the shining path
The Lord's anointing is for soul winning to expand His kingdom
When everyone has heard, the end will come
Everyone looks like Jesus: rich, poor, fat, or skinny
Once born again, they transform from glory to glory

An aversion to poverty is not an aversion to poor people
Jesus died for every person on earth, not just those you see
Many things can distract you, so don't pay attention to them
His anointing comes upon you, and you become more like Him
Dogma, doctrine, and tradition have their place in God's eyes
But can interfere with the anointing if given time

The refreshing is about yielding to Jesus and His way
What worked yesterday is already done, today is a new day
Refreshing is creative and brings something new to the scene
Refreshing is His Spirit: supernatural, powerful, and lovely
Refreshing doesn't come through a formula, isn't calculated
It comes by God's will, according to your heart, so activate it!

No Limits

Inspiration: The Holy Spirit's power is unlimited and God gave believers the authority to use it by invoking the name of Jesus.

> *Scripture:* 1 John 4:4 (NKJV) says, "You are of God, little children, and have overcome them, because He who is in you is greater than he who is in the world."

It is the heart's cry that brings forth healing
That yearning desire from the spirit has meaning
Jesus cannot refuse, nor will He turn His back
Get your heart in line by jerking out the slack

You dabble a little here and there
But haven't brought His power consistently to bear
Turn it on and off at your will, as your heart desires
When your heart cries for others, Jesus shows up as life

The breath of life, that quickening spirit
He's inside you all the time, so take off the limits
Take off the blinders and clean out your ears
You are the one that blocks what you hear

The problem isn't physical, it lies deeper than that
The problem is of the flesh, which is accustomed to combat
The flesh battles, and the mind contemplates
Watching the circumstances and seeing dire straits

Get out of the flesh to bring peace to your heart
Spend time with Jesus, whose presence is where you are
The mountains move, and the earth quakes
Situations in the natural are bonds He breaks

Nothing is greater than God's word, He said it was so
He brings armies forth, angels fall in row upon row
They are your messengers, so use them to do your bidding
Look over the heavenlies and see battles they are winning

They can do more when they follow your commands
The spirit realm is conquered by your words and their hands
When God has your attention, things spring forth
Spend time with the Holy Spirit, it's like visiting the shore

The cool breeze comes and refreshes your spirit
The refreshing comes every time, there is no limit
The soothing calm as gentle as the sea mist
The power builds inside, He's charging you with it

The power generator dwells inside and never sleeps
To hit the gusher of glory and provision, dig deep
The deep abyss where time and space are one
It's where the beginning of creation was

When the spirit and the flesh are one again, it's creation's peak
Rejuvenated, made alive and powerful by the words you speak
Words He sent forth through your spirit as commands
When you walk together again hand-in-hand

For your benefit, for your healing, and into the world
Sail in that power with all your flags unfurled
Catch every breeze to lift you and take you farther
The next level is just beyond where you are, it's not harder

It's not difficult, Jesus made it easy for you
He is working with your flesh, so He had to make it easy to do
It is the heart He searches, and faithfulness He craves
Your consistency and diligence are added to what He gave

He can give the ability to do, the Holy Spirit has all power
He operates as you yield and works through your willpower
It's a fortress, a stronghold, a barrier that must be broken
A house divided cannot stand, the doors must open

Every tragedy and hardship have within them opportunity
When adversity hits, you need wisdom and ingenuity
By God's Spirit and His word you overcome
By His Spirit and His word, Jesus and you become one

God put the mountains here and gave you dominion over them
His Spirit is infallible, He is the power to move them
The power generator that ignites even the flesh
Who quickens dead things and brings light to the darkness

All things are possible to him who believes
Believing limits the scope of your possibilities
Not belief of the head, your mind cannot compare
The vision planted in the heart is the one Jesus brings to bear

Catch the vision and run with it, over and over again
Meditate on it in your mind, come closer to the vision
Grasp it with your hand, touch it, and know it's yours
Don't let that ember die, and the fire will burn its course

When you get to your limit, where you can do no more
Jesus has your next step waiting with Him, He opens the door
The door opens the treasury, His storehouse is vast
He will not only bless you, but others with the net you cast

Quit trying so hard, just live by God's grace
Follow His plan and let go of the reins
Let Jesus steer the sleigh and direct your path
When limits constrain you, the Holy Spirit's got your back

God's Spirit in You

Inspiration: Praying in tongues edifies the believer and makes our spirit more sensitive to the things of the Holy Spirit. Praying in tongues is like priming the pump. Get ready for the overflow!

Scripture: Romans 8:26 (NKJV) says, "Likewise the Spirit also helps in our weaknesses. For we do not know what we should pray for as we ought, but the Spirit Himself makes intercession for us with groanings which cannot be uttered."

Salvation is not about the miracles they do
It is about the Holy Spirit imparted to you
The Holy Spirit gives life to the new creation
The Spirit is the power to change a nation
Hovering over the face of the deep
Tongues of fire filling the hundred and twenty
The Holy Spirit looks over the earth and sees
Spirits of people longing to be free
They are dead and without hope
Without God's Spirit, it is difficult to cope

He leads you, guides you, and beseeches you
His Spirit dwells in you to teach you
To teach you all things about God and His ways
The Holy Spirit abides in you and never strays
If all believers are one in thought, purpose, and action
His power comes to bear, He loves your passion
He cannot stand the thought of anyone left behind
They never leave Him, are always on His mind
Jesus came for those who believe
The Holy Spirit on the inside is what you receive

Inside you, God's Spirit makes His abode
He is changing you and shifting the load
Shifting from the world's way of doing things to His
Like drinking new wine, being filled with His Spirit
When you pray in tongues, the Holy Spirit prays
You may not understand it, it's God's way
It is a sound so sweet to His ear
That heavenly language so sincere
No demon in hell can interfere
Those words are words only God can hear

You do not know what to pray for as you ought
His Spirit helps you, through Him the words are brought
Straight to heaven where God sits on His throne
Before God, where all of the words are known
When you pray in tongues you build, edify, and strengthen
Build on your most holy faith, with Christ as the foundation
His Spirit is inside you and yearns to shine through
Pray in tongues, speak His words, and He will understand you
All things work together for good to those who love Jesus
Intercession is a sweet aroma that strengthens you in weakness

Prayer on earth is the only thing the Holy Spirit responds to
Without intercession many will continue to be bound to
Old habits, old ways of living, and ignorance of God's word
Your prayer provides answers all over the earth
God's Spirit in you will correct and chastise
Filled with His Spirit, by the Spirit you are baptized
Only then can you truly be on one accord
He operates through your flesh, with His sword
The Holy Spirit will change and renew
He cannot enter without making a new you

The Spirit doesn't force you to imitate
He will lead and show you the way
Because He knows God's way is best
And more profitable than all the rest
He will lead you the way of peace
He will bring joy and put your mind at ease
He is the gentle nudge you feel at night
Waking you up to burn your light
To pray for that someone in dire straits
Pray until the burden lifts, your answer awaits

The Holy Spirit in you will bring Jesus to the sinner
The life you live is a light, a glimmer
Jesus is not in the world, but you are there
A platform for Him, His Spirit to share
The Holy Spirit who quickened Christ from the dead
He changes death to life, His Spirit to yours is wed
His Spirit appointed you to the place you are called
The Spirit knows you inside out, He knows it all
He will give you the words to speak in time of need
He is planted inside you as the incorruptible Seed

The Holy Spirit gives gifts to men according to His will
A word received at the right time is an absolute thrill
As the anointing of the Spirit comes upon you
Know He is there to do what God said He would do
Your words demonstrate His power
His power works the works in this final hour
The miracles you do are only for a sign
A sign to the unbeliever that now is the time
Surrender your heart to Jesus, God's Son
Be filled with the Holy Spirit for edification

Go Beyond

Inspiration: There is confusion in the world, with the world's system, and with worldly ways. The mind is influenced by the devil and works toward this confusion. We step outside the world's system with authority in the name of Jesus and the power of the Holy Spirit.

> *Scripture:* John 15:15 (NKJV) says, "No longer do I call you servants, for a servant does not know what his master is doing; but I have called you friends, for all things that I heard from My Father I have made known to you."

It's not only the blind who don't see
You don't need them to be who God wants you to be
Early in the morning you catch the worm
The works of the wicked one cause you to squirm

Your flesh crawls, and your mouth speaks
Your mind meditates and then repeats
It all happens so fast, and then it's gone
Leaving you wondering for so long

God challenges you to go beyond, to dig deep
Go beyond the natural, beyond what you hear and see
Beyond the surreal, beyond the hyperbole
Go beyond the natural, when you step into His reality

It's not only the deaf who don't hear
The sounds of the world cackling in your ear
Don't rely on the senses, they are only a guide
Accurate and adequate if you are led by the light

Otherwise, senses deceive and then persuade
They are busy changing the rules of the game
Been playing so long you don't recognize the fake
Turn the corner, and let Jesus show you God's way

Peace in your heart, His joy's got you dancing
Kick 'em to the curb, the things you've been romancing
Love isn't fickle, or folly, or subject to change
Love is the number one rule in God's game

Jesus is kind and patient and there in your darkest hour
He is firm and unwavering, He strikes with power
The power that drives out sin and shame
The authority comes by speaking the Lord's name

The fruit on that tree was the cross that became
The sin wasn't just forgiven, it was erased
Sin comes through the flesh, watch the veil swoop down
It covers up what's real and obscures the crown

Victory's only a word away
Only say the Name, it's the Lord's name
There is a reality behind what you see
It comes into existence with words that you speak

A chain of events that you never saw coming
You can't stand in place, they keep you running
Where you're going, you don't even know
Can't see what's at the end, just gotta go

What you run from, you don't understand
Like going down a dark alley or sinking in quicksand
What you don't see or hear can kill you
The devils' got a plan, and he'll see it through

He doesn't care about you, he's just laughing
Another one bites the dust, his lips are smacking
Cuz you don't see what you think you see
You don't hear, because you're not listening

You don't trust what you can't feel
Keep going on, like a rat on an exercise wheel
You cry 'heaven, help me,' but don't believe it exists
You hope so, but without seeing it, you can only wish

The world God created didn't look like this
The human being He created is now a misfit
People are afraid to hear the truth
But watch the world suffering on the evening news

Get up out of your seat, and see what God sees
See what He enables you to see
Hear what He enables you to hear
You don't realize it, but the end is drawing near

People say they see the signs, and some of them do
You are not just a spectator, do what He showed you
Jesus Christ opens the door to reality
Go beyond through the Holy Spirit, and see what God sees

The Holy Spirit Works through You

Inspiration: The other day I decided to make some black beans and rice. I took some to my brother, who likes black beans and rice. He told me that his wife was going to be home late from work that night. So he was wondering what he was going to eat for dinner. The Holy Spirit is working even when we don't know He's working. The Holy Spirit works through us as we hear, study, and do the word that we hear. Praise the Lord!

> *Scripture:* 1 Corinthians 12:11 (NKJV) says, "But one and the same Spirit works all these things, distributing to each one individually as He wills."

Did you ever wonder why the Bible wasn't written simply?
Spelled out in plain language and listed categorically?
Jesus could have written it all out while He was here
Would have saved us time to be educated, years and years
God's word is imparted to people by His Spirit
Like Moses who spent forty days and nights on the mountain
David got the plans for the tabernacle from God
He spent time in prayer working things out

Biblical writers got the word the same way you get it
It has always been this way, God hasn't changed His methods
The word is a pearl purchased at a great price
If you never open the oyster, you see only the outside
The shell is nice
The meat is on the inside
You chew on the meat, the meat is for the mature
The pearl has great value, the pearl is God's word

Dig deep inside, and He will reveal
Go deeper into the Holy Spirit, enjoy the whole meal
He wants all of you: body, soul, and spirit
Get engrossed in His word and live every day through Him
You can't get all of Him by having heard
Read, meditate, and ponder His word
As you study, He brings the revelation
Brings you to a new level, beyond damnation

Hear God's word, study His word, and then do
This is how the word becomes embedded in you
Jesus did only what He saw His Father do
He saw God in the Spirit and then followed through
He fasted forty days and nights in the wilderness
He was being prepared by the Holy Spirit for service
Prepared to witness to God, that He is who He said
The disciples saw Jesus alive, before He rose from the dead

Jesus was their example in thought, word, and deed
He came straight from God, He's the incorruptible Seed
The disciples walked with Jesus and watched Him every day
They never saw Him stumble through obstacles in the way
Jesus overcame them by the words He heard His Father speak
He didn't write the Bible, because no one would believe
The false prophets' words are their own witness
The Lord's witness are the works He did while in the flesh

The words Jesus spoke were words from heaven's store
No one on earth had ever spoken like Jesus before
The Holy Spirit imparted wisdom and compassion
And worked miracles through Jesus, that Man of action
The Holy Spirit endued Jesus with power
And then left Him in that final hour
Jesus drank the cup God gave Him, the covenant He kept
His promise to humankind, the Holy Spirit has never slept

His Spirit inspires men the same way today
With glory and power, the Spirit imparts grace
Grace flows from heaven into a bottomless cup
Drink more and more, let the Holy Spirit fill you up
If the revelation isn't coming, it's your fault, not His
He'll show you everything as you spend time in His presence
The word comes by revelation, the same as always
God works through people, He's longsuffering in His ways

He could speak through a donkey again if He needs to
He will do anything to communicate His message to you
He has a personal word for each of His children
Listen for those words, and they will bring abundance
In every area of your life, He has great joy for you
Out of your inner being, His blessings pour through
Jesus could have done a lot of things He didn't do
God gave you the Holy Spirit, so He could work through you

As The Holy Spirit Wills

Inspiration: The Holy Spirit is another of God's precious gifts to the believer. He strengthens us and gives us power to accomplish God's will in the earth realm.

> *Scripture:* Romans 8:1 (NKJV) says, "*There is* therefore now no condemnation to those who are in Christ Jesus, who do not walk according to the flesh, but according to the Spirit."

As the Holy Spirit wills, so contrary to human thought
The Holy Spirit is not a human, He is God
You cannot push Him or force His hand
He operates in God's timing and according to His plan

God's power is always part of the program
The Holy Spirit powers our resurrection
You cannot harness the power of the universe
He set each celestial body as He prefers

There is so much out there that you have never seen
You are only part of the equation, a tiny, fragile human being
But if God's Spirit dwells in you, you are mighty and not weak
You are an overcomer in the blood of Jesus by the words you speak

If you can think of something, the devil can too
He will shoot fiery darts to try to hinder you
God created Lucifer in splendor and glory
But he got caught up in pride and filled with envy

Satan doesn't think like Jesus, he is corrupt
He doesn't know what is next, or where Jesus is coming from
Your brain is magnificent and smarter than a computer
Even the computer learns from people, like with a tutor

The Holy Spirit works in God's timing and always gets it right
That is why you have to walk by faith, and not by sight
God's purpose for you is good, and His plans will be fulfilled
They're already completed in the spirit, according to His will

The Holy Spirit is not a puppet and cannot be manipulated
He is God's gift to humankind, holy and consecrated
The power of salvation for every human being
The Holy Spirit gives us ideas and initiates believing

He is God's hand in the earth realm, who's leading Christ's body
He is freedom from every vice, He's complete liberty
He works from the inside and planted the fruit in you
Nudges you to bring the fruit out, He compels you

He is the power of grace that answers prayers
The Shekinah glory lighting dark places
He wants your complete surrender, give God all of you
He will open you up, pour in the Spirit, and fill you through

God needs yielded vessels, who are willing to go forth
Upon His command, but remember He is the source
You can do nothing of yourself, you're made of only dirt
But when the Holy Spirit works through you, you burst

Burst forth with God's power to move any mountain
With power to open blind eyes and cast out every demon
Speak His will and word and higher you climb
Change those around you by accepting eternal life

The Holy Spirit comes down to your level and builds step-by-step
You start with the right foot and then follow with the left
Don't try to figure Him out, your mind can't handle it
You have to seek Jesus for answers, that's how He planned it

To have intimacy with you, a relationship so close
He dwells inside you, inside you His word grows
He can only give you as much as you will receive
He doesn't control anyone's life, He only leads

He leads you on His path to that place of prosperity
You must be born again to partake of the blessing
The Holy Spirit is like a car, so get in there and rev Him up
You can never move forward without powering up

God's people are destroyed for lack of knowledge, it's true
He has done everything He can do to get His word into you
Without God's word there is no life, only death
Talk to Him every day to get yourself refreshed

Surrender that last little part of yourself completely
There is nothing He holds back from you, except the glory
Humility, appreciation, compassion, and patience
Work them into your spirit to gain inspiration

His timing is perfect, His nature is divine
He created you and anointed you for this time
Fear not, you have not missed His timing
The time is not now, He will enable you to see

The gifts operate to edify the Lord's body
Taking people in from the rain to reality
When a seed enters the ground, it is tiny and round
It doesn't look like that when it breaks through the ground

The seed must be watered and fed, and sunlight acts upon it
If sewn into good ground, you can shortly expect a harvest
Continue your worship, praise, and thanksgiving
Seek Jesus to benefit the body, just keep believing

God manifests Himself in many ways, according to His word
Can't put your finger on Him, the timing not deferred
He doesn't confirm your ministry or your office
God confirms His word, and His word always profits

SECTION 4

Poems about the power of God's word And its effect on our daily lives

"Rejoice! Jesus gave you the victory, you have already won
Do not be troubled and do not be afraid, the works are done"

Crooked Places

"The sword is God's word, slice the devil up like cherry pie
Don't let him stick around long enough to ask you why"

Dominion and Seed

Why We Do the Things We Do

Inspiration: Adam disobeyed God by eating the fruit of the tree of the knowledge of good and evil. Adam gave attention to what the serpent said. In doing so, he gave the serpent authority to speak into his life; in effect, turning his allegiance to the serpent. We are all descendants of Adam, so the serpent still has authority to speak into our lives today. That is, until and unless we receive Jesus as our personal Lord and Savior. In Jesus, we have authority over the devil once again. Hallelujah!

> *Scripture:* 1 John 3:8 (NKJV) says, "He who sins is of the devil, for the devil has sinned from the beginning. For this purpose the Son of God was manifested, that He might destroy the works of the devil."

People wonder why you do the things you do
They don't understand, it's the Lord who's calling you
He called you to fulfill His plan
His ways are higher than those of man
You get out of the boat and begin to walk
The others in the boat begin to talk
They see the wind, they see the wave
And stay in the boat because they are afraid

People are born into the world under sin
Under the sway of the wicked one, who dwells within
He wants to confine you to the natural realm
Death is your end with Satan at the helm
You operate in the things the mind can conceive
Your emotions, friends, and families lead
You have the traditions of the world to guide you
Principalities, powers, and dominions smite you

Sickness and disease, famine and pestilence
The curse of the law is your death sentence
Poverty and lack, hatred and death
You struggle to survive and fight to the end
Dying a little on the inside every day
Knowing there has to be another way
The devil will give some of you real wealth
Don't think of anyone else, just take care of yourself

He will give you all your desires, all the best
It is all a deception, in him there is no rest
You cannot sleep, and you eat too much
You trust no one, because they're just after your stuff
They steal your ideas and cheat on their wife
Couldn't you just have one day without any strife?
The rest you seek will never come
You're on the wrong path, following the wrong one

You read the horoscope and dangle a charm
Thinking these things can't do you any harm
New age religions, witches, and magicians
Called by many names, but still the same mission
Every day it seems there is something else
But there is no forgiveness, it is all about self
They do not proclaim theirs is the way to eternal life
Even they know only Jesus gives everlasting light

Satan knows he's wrong, and that he loses in the end
He keeps doing his job, he is persistent
As the author of confusion, he pokes and prods
He wants you to do evil by serving other gods
Jealousy, hunger, and greed are from the enemy
So are poverty, abuse, and materiality
God gives us all the choice to make
Do we want death or life? Eternal life is at stake

Make no bones about it, God's word is true
What He says will happen, will come upon you
Your thirst is not quenched, and the worm doesn't die
When you go to hell, your soul remains alive
You live forever, tortured and burned
Regretting your choices, and wishing you had learned
What Jesus tells you is true, that people live forever
The spirit does not die, nor is the mind is severed

Whether you like it or not, doesn't change the truth
Satan is a liar, but don't think he's stupid
He was the angel who covered, an anointed cherubim
He was the most beautiful of all, just ask him
He exalted himself above God's throne
He was so proud, heaven was his home
Jesus saw him fall like lightening from the sky
Sin has no place in God's presence, gets seared by fire

Satan will forever burn in the lake of fire
He rules for now, expanding his earthly empire
Harassing and confusing you, he never tells the truth
He stole your inheritance from you in your youth
This poem is not about glorifying him
But to expose him for what he is, to reveal him
And to tell you that way back in the beginning of time
God had a plan, you were always on His mind

The division created between the serpent and the woman
Between her Seed and his, was perfected in salvation
That division came through Jesus, God's Son
Through Jesus Christ, you have redemption
He came in the flesh and lived a human being as we
Baptized in the Jordan by the Holy Spirit, with authority
He had all the power of God when He walked the earth
Casting out the devil with only a word

Well, not just any word, but the word of God
Satan is under Christ's feet, like a dirt clod
The blood that Jesus shed on the cross
The day of the Lord's death was the start of Satan's loss
Jesus died and was buried, but rose again
After He defeated Satan and conquered sin
Three days in hell the devil danced with glee
But God's Spirit raised Jesus up and gave Him the victory

That victory He confers upon you in salvation
You are more than conquerors once you accept Jesus
God respects your opinion, He lets you choose
Walk in death with Satan, whose goal is to confuse
Or choose life in Jesus, and your spirit is renewed
His peace and joy come to dwell inside you
Through Jesus, you stand before God as though you had no sin
Through Jesus, every sin in your life has been forgiven

Jesus is out there on the water, He doesn't need the boat
Look closely above the wave, and you'll see He is afloat
The ordinary things that people can do
Are not the things Jesus came to do
Jesus came to bring life more abundantly
He comes to dwell inside you, will you receive?
He offers you life in heaven with God eternally
Living on the earth, in Jesus you have the victory

Free

Inspiration: God trusts us so much that He created us with free will. He gave us His word and His power to create. We succeed or fail based on our own words and actions. That's power.

> *Scripture:* Hebrews 4:12 (NKJV) says, "For the word of God *is* living and powerful, and sharper than any two-edged sword, piercing even to the division of soul and spirit, and of joints and marrow, and is a discerner of the thoughts and intents of the heart."

Walk with Jesus, His burden is light
His word will make you want to walk right
The Holy Spirit is planted, God's word is there too
The anointing grows stronger as the word comes through

Death and life are in the power of the tongue
Speak the words He gives you, from your heart they come
The word is medicine, it is health to your flesh
The anointing is in the word that you confess

You will have what you say, your words are power
For death or life, they build or destroy the tower
The foundation is laid, who is Jesus Christ, God's Son
Through authority in His name, the works are done

The power was vested in Jesus as head of the church
He sat down at God's right hand after all sin was purged
The closer you get to the Spirit, the closer He gets to you
Sin is bondage, a yoke around your neck, I'm telling you

Satisfy yourself in Jesus, He's all you'll ever need
Cast your burdens on Him and then proceed with your dreams
The vision in your heart, God put it there
Eyes firmly fixed on the word, believe Him, do you dare?

The treasures He has are all abundance
He says 'Yes' and 'Amen' to all the promises
The flesh is the snare that has you bogged down in habits
Traditions are man-made and can keep you from God's best

Showers of spiritual blessings fall upon your head
Keep your flesh under subjection by acting like it's dead
Sin causes death to something and disrupts the vision
The devil and his devices are trying to hinder your mission

At the end of the day, God's word is all you have
His word separates the wheat from the chaff
He's pruning the vine, separating death from life
The word quickens dead things, is powerful and alive

If you need finances, just tell them to come
Relationship troubles? God's word is wisdom
Speak to the mountain, by His word it moves
Peace and joy flood your spirit when you worship in truth

The life in Jesus, where everything is whole
Flesh is a glass half empty, the Holy Spirit fills it full
Come up to God's throne, your praise floods His senses
That sweet aroma is praise without pretenses

When your heart is full of Jesus, the flesh won't satisfy
He and the Father come to dwell, in you They abide
Don't treat Them as a guest staying two or three weeks
They transform at the cellular level, firm like concrete

Time in God's presence builds you higher and higher
Like an edifice, when His will becomes your desire
Seek only Jesus, and then everything else will fall in place
He opens His arms and showers comfort and grace

To be or not to be is a question people ask
In Jesus you live forever, anointed for your task
Rules and regulations come because of sin
Love is His only law, and it's working from within

He transforms you as your heart is born from above
You are His children, not of flesh, but of love
He will speak to you again, but will you receive?
He is talking all the time to those who believe

He teaches you the word and brings it to your remembrance
Walking in the word is walking in blessings
The flesh gets in the way, so it must be crucified
All sin was abolished with the death Jesus died

He declared you righteous, in Him you have an inheritance
Works don't get you saved, give Jesus preeminence
He wipes away the sin but leaves your free will in tact
He created you in His image, and He will not take it back

He wants you to choose Him, not to be His slave
The Israelites knew God's acts, but Moses knew His ways
The gifts of the Spirit are His acts even today
They operate through love, love is His way

Walk in love and let it swell up in your heart
Love crushes flesh and gives it no part
When you love something, hold it close and don't let go
Love builds and strengthens, it's more valuable than gold

With sin in your life, love takes a back seat
You respond to the flesh and forget about reality
The devil is behind all sin, but you call the shots
Sin hinders prayers, like setting up roadblocks

You cry out to Jesus, and then He shows you the problem
Cast your problems on Him, He loves to solve them
The truth of the matter is there is only one way to be free
Get to the place where you fall in love with Jesus completely

Glory Proclaimed

Inspiration: This poem talks about the tricks of Satan and how to overcome them by using the authority in the name of Jesus and the power of the Holy Spirit. In Jesus, all sin is forgiven. Praise and worship are music to God's ears and a weapon against Satan's tricks.

> *Scripture:* Hebrews 2:14 (NKJV) says, "Inasmuch then as the children have partaken of flesh and blood, He Himself likewise shared in the same, that through death He might destroy him who had the power of death, that is, the devil."

God's word is for the entire world to hear
The devil knows the end is drawing near
He is not stupid as some choose to believe
He knows the pit of fire is the punishment he receives

He knows the time is limited for him to rule
Perfect in the day he was made, he occupied God's throne room
He was in the Garden of Eden, puffed up and vain
He exalted himself, his ego he refused to contain

Bounced out of heaven like a ball
Fell to earth in a tumultuous fall
He bears the scar of the battle he lost
Got the right foot of fellowship and was tossed

Down to the earth he went, angry and seeking revenge
He preys on God's creation, He's jealous of the sons of men
There is nothing good in him, He's twisted like a candy cane
No longer beautiful to behold, when he fell, God changed his name

He plays the same game year after year
He has never created anything, just stirs up fear
Fear in the hearts of men who don't know their authority
Jesus Christ is God's Son, He obtained the victory

The devil rules the earth, but Jesus has the keys
Jesus defeated the devil, Death, and Hades
He did it for you, for every sinner to be saved
Pull away from Satan's grasp when you believe on the Lord's name

No, Satan's not stupid, He always uses the same tricks
They work every time, so there's no need to switch
The flesh is weak, and there he attacks
Flesh is never born again, integrity it lacks

The mind is the devil's playground and is not renewed
Thoughts from the enemy are cunning and must be subdued
Pour the word into your heart like water into a glass
God's word is a defense against the devil's attacks

If Satan confronted Jesus, he'll tempt you too
Like a dripping faucet, he keeps coming after you
He comes for the saints and not just for the sinners
He already rules sinners' hearts as the default winner

Adam's disobedience was submission to Satan's lordship
Not heeding God's word, obedience is worship
Through Adam, every person on earth is born into sin
Accept Jesus Christ as Lord and get a better inheritance

Receive eternal life and stand before God in righteousness
Forget the sin, it is forgiven, come into His presence
A relationship with each person is God's greatest desire
The devil wants to drag you down with him to the pit of fire

The devil can only overtake you if you refuse the Lord's name
Even if you bow to temptation, once saved, you are saved
God's mercy is boundless, He forgives you every day
He sees you through Jesus Christ, who is the only way

When you receive Jesus as Lord, you receive His robe
With wisdom, righteousness, and sanctification you are clothed
The crown on His head is on your head too
Look at yourself through the mirror God uses

Every hair on your head is numbered, He loves you that much
Satan is under your feet, Jesus grabbed you from his clutch
The dread of darkness is lifted, just enjoy His light
Confusion is not from God, so refuse it outright

The devil has been overcome but don't underestimate him
He's a relentless foe, but don't let him get you frustrated
When you speak God's word, he runs from you in terror
Eventually he will avoid you, because Jesus is his bad news bearer

The devil flees from God's word, doesn't want to lose any ground
Jesus' name casts him out, praise and worship spin him around
Satan wants the worship and the glory
That pretty much sums up his story

Worship Jesus, the devil cannot stand the sound
He must flee from praise, and thanksgiving confounds
Continue in God's presence, where the anointing flows
Where peace and joy are, your relationship grows

Stronger and closer and more intimate
Send the sacrifice of praise, then God releases the worship
There is power in praise, God stands up to take notice
Praise is music to His ears, so get into His presence

It is the only sacrifice He requires you to give
Mountains move with the fruit of your lips
The devil is like a caged lion, seeking whom he may devour
He stored up his greatest fury for this, the final hour

The end will not come until everyone has heard
Satan's firing all cylinders to divert attention from God's word
As the end draws near, the battles become more aggressive
Throwing everything he's got at once, he's that desperate

But you, child of God, have authority in the name of Jesus
God's glory is proclaimed when you stand in His presence
You can do all things, because He strengthens you
Jesus won the victory, and then He gave it to you

Turn Pages

Inspiration: When you're down and out, Jesus is still
Lord and His word still has power. I started this poem
out of my spirit, my soul really, about how I was feeling
at the time. Then the Holy Spirit took over at "Jesus is
not a theory, a concept nor a silly notion." Whoa!

> *Scripture:* Romans 6:4 (NKJV) says, "Therefore we were buried
> with Him through baptism into death, that just as Christ was
> raised from the dead by the glory of the Father, even so we also
> should walk in newness of life."

Broken and empty and confused and lost
Willing to do what You asked, no matter the cost
Weakened in the knees, but strengthened in spirit
Wisdom and understanding, wanting more than is given

Torn and crushed, the blows kept falling
Wanting the storm to pass, just started walking
I don't know the direction, and I'm not seeing any signs
Just rolling forward, I'm rolling with the times

Can't really go forward on my own, only from side-to-side
The directions keep changing, so I start toeing the line
I'm circling around, the purpose I don't see
Hearing crazy ideas, like salvation on a tree

The course is straight, but the path is crooked
Trying to make it my own, I gotta keep looking
Got my nose to the ground, looking this way and that
Looking for love, but only hearing ratta-tat-tat-tat

The sound of the machine gun firing away at my head
The heart is in there too, please don't forget
Not made of stone or metal or iron
It slows and stumbles at times, but keeps firing

Take it or leave it, you only get what you give
I take stock of the emotions, they're leaking like a sieve
Confusion all around, getting no answers at church
Try changing behavior, the theory that never worked

Jesus is not a theory, a concept, nor a silly notion
He is the truth, and His words move in forward motion
The words He speaks are full of understanding
All wisdom in His words, always a safe landing

Keep looking for knowledge, it all started with God
It is made in Him, for Him, and through Him, look at Jesus
You can't see, if you're never gonna look
You'll never understand, if you don't open the Book

God's word has power, backed by heaven's throne
His love is pouring out, so you'll never be alone
The law was a tutor, teaching you how to behave
But real power conquered death and conquered the grave

That's right, death is done away with, it's eternally finished
It will never rise again, its power completely diminished
Jesus brings new life, He gives it freely and holds nothing back
It's more than changing behavior, it's not just overcoming lack

The super bowl plays every year, lotsa people watch it
It's quite a spectacle, few things in the world match it
They replay the game year after year, always a new champion
Jesus rose from the grave, conquered death, never to die again

Once for all, all sin wiped completely clean
Jesus was there in beginning, at the end He'll still be standing
At the Father's right hand, He is bathed in glory
Forget behavior modification, the life of Jesus is the real story

His life and His death, a story like none other
He opened heaven's doors, He welcomes all His brothers
You are His brothers when you confess His name
Jesus comes to live inside you, and your life is never the same

He uproots the experiences and reconfigures your compass
Engulfs you and embraces you, He doesn't care about your past
Forget the shame, because life is much more than circumstances
The binding that bound you binds no more, it's time for advances

Plod and plow and trudge through the depths
Heaven's doors are open to you, so get out of the mess
Focus on Jesus and behold His image, He is the way
He's eternal and unchangeable, yesterday, tomorrow, and today

No need for confusion, so just put it down and walk away
As long as you keep holding on, He will not let you go astray
Behold the image and then follow Jesus, the way you will know
Turn the page, turn over a new leaf, and then get up and go

If you focus on you or focus on the flesh, they will take you down
Like treading water and losing strength, you start to drown
God's word is where the power is, and you can never get enough
When the devil tries to pull you down again, just call his bluff

Shake 'Em Up

Inspiration: Believers have been given authority in the name of Jesus to overcome the works of the devil. When we use it, we shake up the kingdom of darkness.

> *Scripture:* Acts 4:31 (NKJV) says, "And when they had prayed, the place where they were assembled together was shaken; and they were all filled with the Holy Spirit, and they spoke the word of God with boldness."

The kingdom of heaven suffers violence
There is no victory without consequence
You must be aggressive and take it by force
Do not be afraid, challenge at the source
Satan is not going to just cave in and give up
He must be confronted at the onset, shaken

God's words supply the force, they are energy
Like flipping a switch to get electricity
Your words are power for good or evil
Be careful what you say, only say what you believe
Words can be darts, and though they may be true
They should only edify, exhort, and comfort you

God's word is reliable, it will stand the test of time
Patience, child of God, is gold in the kingdom He designed
Confessions are important and so is prayer
If you do not rest on your laurels, you will be safer
Move out on His word and live each day as new
Don't get stuck in a rut, just let the word refresh you

God's word brings rest if it is applied
Rest is for doers, and not just in the sweet bye-and-bye
Rest is confidence, knowing you are in His perfect will
A bridge over stormy waters, the waters are stilled
He told you His yoke is easy, and His burden is light
Don't struggle in the flesh, walk by faith, not by sight

The principalities, powers, and prince of the power of the air
Tempt your flesh and nip at your heels, they do not fight fair
You don't need to fight, because Jesus gave you the victory
He gave you His name with all heaven's authority
Command them to move, and they get out of your way
There is upset in the spirit realm, Satan's realm is shaken

Shake 'em up, shake 'em up, shake 'em up, shake 'em
The works are waiting to be done, to be undertaken
Do not look to the left or to the right and do not doubt
This is a prize fight, so stand'em up and knock'em out
Call it like you see it, but give the devil no place
Every believer must confront him by getting in his face

He lurks around, looking for a sign of weakness
Fill your cup to the brim overflowing in Jesus
Make no room for the devil, so that he cannot get in
Build yourself up in God's word to get the refreshing
Step out in confidence in the boldness He gave you
Stand up straight and get in his face, Jesus will not forsake you

Your lamp stand receives a ceaseless flow of oil
A tree stands tall in the forest, planted in good soil
Soil needs fertilizer, water, and sunshine to produce
God's word nourishes and strengthens you when put to use
Trying is not doing, first you must believe
You cannot believe what you have not received

True peace can be yours by authority in the Lord's name
It is yours to use, and Jesus will not be put to shame
The deceiver's time on earth is coming to a close
Kick him out of your life now, and out he goes
The name of Jesus heals the sick of every disease
The suffering doesn't have to continue, please

Get out there and bring in His harvest
Take His light to the world in darkness
They have been there so long, they don't even know it
Don't let complacency rule in your heart, but overthrow it
So many sinners and so little time
Preach God's word, it changes lives

Any area of lack in your life Jesus has already overcome
Taking authority over it in His name is how it's done
Money is necessary to spread the gospel to the earth
Abraham didn't get the riches until after he left Ur
The covenant was established when he offered Isaac, his son
God's covenant is tested by people, but can never be broken

Finances come, ministering angels retrieve them for you
They are awaiting your command to tell them what to do
The covenant is God's love and the Holy Spirit with all His power
The animal skins provided Adam with spiritual cover
Blood covered his transgression, the blood of animals
The blood of Jesus cleanses, it's established once for all

Surrender yourself to the Holy Spirit, and He does the rest
The evidence of His Spirit is power, He is the greatest
The devil won't give up easily, he is cunning
You have authority in the name of Jesus, use it to stun him
The victory has been given to you through Jesus
Shake 'em up, shake 'em up, shake 'em up, shake 'em

Crooked Places

Inspiration: The traps of the devil lead us into crooked places.
Use the word against them. Use the authority in the name
of Jesus against them. Build your spirit up by spending time
in God's word and in the Holy Spirit to overcome them.

> *Scripture:* Isaiah 45:2 (NKJV) says, "'I will go before you And
> make the crooked places straight; I will break in pieces the
> gates of bronze And cut the bars of iron.'"

Death and life are in the power of the tongue, it's true
Do not worry, child of God, the blood of Jesus is covering you
Words have power, but if they are not His will
They fall into the devil's lap, his wishes fulfilled
They are in his playing field, the devil plays the game
The words have power once spoken, and not for your gain
Satan cannot block your path, but can hinder your steps
Be careful what you speak, or the devil profits

The words enter the atmosphere and cause confusion
Satan has a right to fulfill them once you use them
That is why God gave you His word to speak
His words comfort, edify, and exhort the believer
God's word, when spoken, eliminates the curse
Through confession of Jesus, you experience the new birth
With your words you step into the spirit realm
Misspoken words open the door for the devil

Guard your heart and only share your secrets with Jesus
Be careful what you say and give the devil no freedom
Rebuke those false prophets and make the correction known
They spoke publicly, but do not let them get a foothold
The Holy Spirit is not dead, but alive forever
Grace covers the believers in the new covenant
Noise is not power, the devil's not afraid of you
He stands up and takes notice when the name of Jesus is used

Keep in line with God's word, so the darts cannot penetrate
Satan nips at your heels, but cast him out and celebrate
His reign is for a time, and then the second death comes
You are redeemed from the curse, Jesus brought redemption
Rejoice! Jesus gave you the victory, you have already won
Do not be troubled and do not be afraid, the works are done
Completed from the foundation of the earth
On the seventh day, God rested from all His works

The Holy Spirit leads the body and each member individually
Grace pours from heaven like manna, just receive
Do not look to the left, do not look to the right
Darkness and light are the same, to God there is no night
Only daytime, bright, bold, beautiful sunshine
The word edifies, it's planted in your heart as a sign
His word was planted in you when you were born again
Faith comes by hearing, hear it over and over again

If the words do not edify, they are not from God
Believers must take authority, witchcraft is rebellion
You can shout at the devil, he won't run
Authority must be spoken in the name of Jesus
The devil is like a wounded animal, backing into a corner
He's hissing and spitting, but you are an overcomer
Overcome him by God's word in every area of lack
Satan stole from you, but by your words you get it back

God's word makes the crooked places straight
If confusion surrounds you, cast it out in the Lord's name
His word will always leave you in a state of peace
The word corrects you and fills you abundantly
With love and joy, comfort and rest
That's why it's important to confess
Fill your cup to overflowing by talking to Jesus in the Spirit
It's the method God gave you, and it works to your benefit

Sing songs, hymns, and psalms, sing from your heart
When you overflow, the devil gets no part
God's word is the answer, Jesus always shows you the way
Seek His face, because He has a word for you today
Judge the prophets and pray only according to God's will
Sheep must not be led astray, but by waters still
Filled with knowledge which leads to wisdom
God's word must be laid as the foundation

Sheep eat in green pastures with no care for their safety
They dine at a table God sets before their enemies
Jesus is the good shepherd, He cares for His sheep
Sheep hear His voice and follow Him closely
Some hear the voice of Jesus, but then they twist it
Their motives are wrong, born of selfish ambition
Some create desires of their heart not in line with the word
The power of those words, when spoken, is transferred

Cancel those plans for your life by authority in the Lord's name
Wayward and cause damage, cancel them in His name
God doesn't bring confusion but a message of liberty
He doesn't bring guilt or condemnation, but identity
Jesus leads you to a place of lasting peace
The fruit of the spirit is planted as a seed
Life in God's word brings the fruit to the surface
When they are exhibited, you fulfill His purpose

Be careful to discern each word that you hear
Do not flood your hearts with pollution, guard your ear
If you don't know God's will, you are in a dangerous place
Come closer to Jesus and accept His loving embrace
You can't hear the word if you're not listening
Another avenue for the devil, overcome it with God's vision
His path for you is lighted and comes straight to His throne
It is clear cut and full of blessing and made of gold

Doers of God's Word

Inspiration: The disciples witnessed Jesus directly and
followed His example. Blessed are those who haven't seen
Jesus in person, yet believe in Him and follow His example.

> *Scripture:* John 14:12 (NKJV) says, "'Most assuredly, I say to
> you, he who believes in Me, the works that I do he will do also;
> and greater *works* than these he will do, because I go to My
> Father."

Doers of God's word are blessed, and not hearers only
Faith comes by hearing, so hear the Lord's testimony
It's about the Holy Spirit leading you to freedom
Your life is like a house of cards without Jesus

Burden upon burden, weight upon weight
Why, oh child of God, do you not cooperate?
The peace of the world is not a lasting peace
It is based on circumstances, not identity

Identifying with Christ and His substitution
You have the same authority that God gave His Son
He didn't create you to bear the world's burdens
As a result of Adam's fall came the world system

Doing God's word puts you in line spiritually
To function as a member of Christ's body
Doing His word brings blessings abundantly
Overflowing lavishly and extravagantly

Obedience is better than sacrifice
The sacrifice of Jesus was once for all time
Follow His example, He knew the word
He did only those things which He heard

He did not operate in the earth as the Son of God
Jesus had flesh to deal with, so They had conversations
He spent all night in prayer and then named His disciples
He prayed in Gethsemane and then gave Himself to be crucified

Jesus told His disciples to watch and pray
But they fell asleep when temptation drew them away
They didn't have the Holy Spirit then, they weren't born again
But were there at Pentecost, and spoke in tongues

They accepted Jesus and then led the way
They did signs and wonders and preached every day
They believed because they saw the miracles Jesus did
Blessed are they who have never seen, and yet enlist

Jesus knew God's will by spending time in prayer
He was changing the world, layer upon layer
When the seventy returned from healing the sick
The Bible recorded that Jesus rejoiced in His spirit

They had become doers of the word, and not just hearers
They used authority in the name of Jesus, their mission clear
Jesus did only what He saw His Father in heaven do
His disciples copied what they saw Jesus do

They operated in the sense realm in what their minds conceived
Blessed are they that have not seen Jesus and yet believe
You do greater works than these because Jesus went to His Father
The works you do because of the word that you have nurtured

You have never seen Jesus, and yet you believe
Based solely on somebody else's testimony
Jesus knew His Father from the beginning of time
Watching His every move, from right by His side

They were always of the same Spirit, so Jesus knew He could do
All the things He saw God do, those things He was a witness to
You have witnessed nothing and yet believe in your heart
That requires belief and action, great faith on your part

God delights to hear you speak His word
He delights to see you do the word
The world and its ways take you so far away from what's real
So far you don't recognize His voice when He speaks

Listening for God's word is one thing
Hearing His word is another thing
Believing the word is yet another thing
Doing God's word is the greatest thing

Dominion and Seed

Inspiration: We reign as kings on earth because of what Jesus did for us. We are not ignorant of the devil's devices, nor of the ways of the world system. We overcome them by the power of the Holy Spirit and authority in the name of Jesus, God's Son.

> *Scripture:* 1 Peter 1:23 (AMP) says, "You have been regenerated (born again), not from a mortal origin (seed, sperm), but from one that is immortal by the *ever* living and lasting Word of God."

God's word is a sword and a seed
The sword cuts down everything that misleads
The seed is to be planted and watered
Dominion and seed were given before the garden
Adam was the ruler of the earth, his wife from his side
Just tend and keep the garden, the place where you abide

Everything you need is here, talk to God during the day
Do not eat of the tree of knowledge, and here you will stay
You could have eaten of the tree of life and lived forever
Satan tempted you, sin corrupted you, and you fell together
God made you like Them, in Their image and likeness
Look in the mirror and see Their reflected presence

God has no sin or sickness, nor is there any in heaven
Satan fell to earth like lightning and fell out of God's presence
Satan is a created being, he was one of God's archangels
But when pride filled him, he became disdainful
Satan doesn't look like God and doesn't understand His ways
He was banished from the throne room, on God's creation he preys

You know all his devices, so get your defenses up
Know that he has already been defeated by Jesus
Have no fear, use the name of Jesus, and send the message clear
Remind the devil of his place, send him running in high gear
His position is under your feet, crawling on the ground
Praise and worship God, the devil cannot stand the sound

The sword is God's word, slice the devil up like cherry pie
Don't let him stick around long enough to ask you why
The seed is God's word, and it's planted in your heart
It flourishes when watered, it takes water to start
The water of the Holy Spirit, who is holy and all powerful
The source of life in the garden, making things grow

Give Jesus an open door, He brings life to the dead
You cannot understand how it works, so get that out of your head
God is tired of seeing His children living in defeat
They must know that in Christ they have the victory
Victory in every area of life, sickness was defeated on the cross
Spiritual death no longer has dominion over you, Satan's lost

Poverty is not a blessing or a sign of humility, it's just ignorance
It's like you rolled over to die, but your body isn't dead yet
Dazed and confused and letting the devil run your life
Kick him to the curb and flood your existence with light
The light is God's word, He will never fail you
Do you believe that, or do you only want to?

You reign as kings, you are God's crowning glory
His life blood is in you, and His substance is holy
You were changed in an instant when you accepted salvation
You cannot be defeated, because the battle is already won
Hold your head high, look around to see everything that's yours
God made it all for you to tend and keep, He opened the doors

The cattle on a thousand hills are His, and you inherited them
Through Jesus, God's Son, take back what was stolen
Seek Jesus and seek His presence, He has a plan for you
To fulfill your destiny and to feed and equip the body too
You cannot follow the world's ways, you are no longer like them
God's substance was transmitted to you, which is His very presence

His nature dwells inside you and is perpetuating the kingdom
You walk by revelation now and not by the world's information
Jesus has better information, the Creator knows the created
Like sailing on smooth seas, your every breath is anticipated
He makes you rich and gives you no sorrow
He lives in eternal now with no tomorrows

He knows the things you have need of before you ask
He guides you to the place you need to be when following His plans
Each step He gives you, go out and get it done
There is an appointed time to run with the vision
The world has its ways, but they fail every time
There were designed to fail, to get you to toe the line

To follow your head and not your heart
To focus on yourself, which is a bad start
There is no eternal life in the world, so it will fade away
Only God's glory overcomes darkness, only His light remains
In an instant, in the twinkling of an eye
You cannot see it now, but Jesus will bring it by

God said it, and He will bring it to pass
It is a minor thing, this thing that you ask
Nothing is too much for God's children
He created it for you when He gave you seed and dominion
It's your heart that He sees, has it been established?
Do you really trust Him, is all unbelief banished?

Fear is from the devil, he made it, it's his composition
It's contrary to faith, faith and fear are in opposition
In faith there is no doubt, so believe what you say
Believing in your heart pushes mountains out of your way
It is not a gimmick, but how God created the worlds
How you got saved in the first place, by this new birth

You are born again, and your spirit is new
Your flesh remains the same and must be renewed
The flesh and the spirit war to gain preeminence
Build yourself up in other tongues and get into God's presence
The flesh and the mind have controlled you since you were born
Putting them under is a process, but old habits must be shorn

God's kingdom is led and managed by His Spirit
Jesus is at His right hand, ministering from heaven
He won't deal with the flesh, which is left to you
The devil gains entry through the flesh, he's always troubling you
But you control him, you have authority in the Lord's name
All spirits are subject to you, your authority is the same

You are Christ's body on earth, nothing happens unless you do it
Satan has dominion over the earth, so you must press through it
Push him back, God's word clears the path
His word has the power to take everything back
Jesus conquered the devil and took away the keys
In the name of Jesus you have dominion, His word is the seed

God's Word

Inspiration: This is one of the first poems that the Holy Spirit dictated to me. It rhymes, has rhythm, and it teaches. It has a special place in my heart. The word can be applied to every area of our lives.

> *Scripture:* John 1:1 (NKJV) says, "In the beginning was the Word, and the Word was with God, and the Word was God."

No word is void, God's word is true
He said He would never lie to you
From His word He never strays
Live by His word every day

God's word is love, His word is power
Divides and conquers in this final hour
His word is eternal, His word is a sword
The word is violent and takes by force

God's word is a comfort to the sick and depressed
His word brings peace to a heart under stress
The word is joy which comes in the morning
His word is calm when the sea is storming

God's word overcomes, His word empowers
His word strengthens you and never cowers
His word is not slack, on His word you can depend
The word will transform you to the very end

God's word builds, and His word chastises
His word corrects, there are no compromises
His word is His Spirit, the giver of life
The word in the darkness is the light

God's word is a fire that consumes
His word is all-knowing, but never presumes
His word will show you the way
The word in you prospers day by day

God's word anoints
His word appoints
His word approves
The word never moves

God's word is the light, eternal in the sky
His word breathes the breath of life
His word will condemn the wicked
The word is how all sins are forgiven

God's word brings faith by hearing it
His word builds compassion by rearing it
His word compels you to action
The word gives the devil no satisfaction

God's word does not faint, nor grows weary
His word is bold, but never leery
His word divides between joint and marrow
The word enters through the gate that is narrow

God's word says ask, and you shall receive
His word says come near, He supplies every need
His word says Jesus will open when you knock
He knows your every move, you are no shock

God's word says seek, and you will find
His word says you are important in His mind
His word is love, and His word is mercy
The word is compassion and is always worthy

God's word is for every person, saint and sinner
His word in you will make you a winner
His word overcomes the darts of the enemy
The word conquered the one who deceives

God's word is so deep, one cannot comprehend
His word is enduring, even from end-to-end
His word enlightens, but no one understands
God's words and ways are higher than any man's

God's word gave all authority to you
His word in the earth is for you to do
His word causes you to act
The word is all true, it's all fact

God's word is filled with the sacrifice of praise
His word compels every hand to be raised
His word wants you to worship Him
The word is solely deserving of the glory

God's word, by which the worlds were framed
The word by which every person is saved
The word declares that He is almighty
The First and the Last, Jesus is the key

God's word is righteous
His word is victorious
His word is enlightening
The word is glorious

God's word came in the flesh
Jesus Christ of Nazareth
His word and Jesus are the same
There is salvation in no other name

Read God's word every day
Pray His word every day
Hear His word every day
Apply the word every day

Poems about prayer to accomplish God's word in our lives and the lives of others

"You are a precious jewel, created in the rough
Buffed and polished and formed perfectly by His love"

Master Stroke

"God knows your intents and purposes because He sees all
Praise and worship are the ultimate battle call"

Battle Call

Master Stroke

Inspiration: The Holy Spirit gave me this poem one night
in corporate intercessory prayer. There was a man with
a deep baritone voice who was unabashed, probably
not realizing how the sound of his voice resonated and
reverberated throughout the room. Boom! Boom! Boom!

> *Scripture:* 2 Corinthians 10:3 (NKJV) says, "For though we
> walk in the flesh, we do not war according to the flesh."

Boom! Boom! Boom!
Prayer fills the room
You cannot comprehend God's timing or His ways
He leads you by the Holy Spirit, alive forever and for always
The demons tremble, and the earth shakes
They recognize the authority and flee in the Lord's name

You fight in the Spirit, not according to the flesh
Prayer is the sweet aroma that fills heaven with incense
Be bold in the name of Jesus, that tool He gave you
He will never leave you, nor will He ever forsake you
God's word is the mantle, see the blood on the doorposts
His seed is planted inside you, by prayer it grows

God is not perfunctory, obligatory, or compulsory
Seeking Him should be your desire, seek Him with urgency
Jesus only ever needed a few
With His power they are endued
They do what He needs them to do, as His word goes forth
Endurance comes from Jesus, His Spirit is the source

You will never hear from God if you are not listening
Works take so little effort with His Spirit's quickening
He will complete the work He started in you
Building in you a desire to do what He needs you to do
To accomplish God's purpose in the earth
Pay attention to Jesus, hear His words

God shows you to her in her prayer time
You are always on His mind
You are a precious jewel, created in the rough
Buffed and polished and formed perfectly by His love
Grace and power implanted until you overflow
Prayer releases the power of Jesus for believers to take control

Press in, and the anointing will flow
When you are on one accord, His body grows
Strife and divisions are works of the flesh
Fueled by pride and fear and demonic spirits
Jesus gave you authority over them in His word
He gave you the victory when you received the new birth

Come boldly into God's presence to the throne of grace
Break forth in hymns, worship, thanksgiving, and praise
He is God, He is God all by Himself
His works can be accomplished by no one else
You hear Him when He speaks, and then you do
You will be blessed in all your ways, God's promise to you

Exceedingly, abundantly, beyond what you ask or think
Consistency in prayer is the missing link
Prayer is a conversation, God listens when you speak
Then you listen to Jesus when He speaks
He has a word that is personal for you
Get His word every day, He will see you through

God created the earth and sent the rain down
He sent forth the blessing and gave you the crown
Grace pours from heaven as a continuous flow
It is the power of the Holy Spirit to give you hope
Grace answers prayers spoken by faith
Grace moves mountains out of your way

Burn the candle at both ends to accomplish
To get what you want, it's a work of the flesh
His yoke is easy, and His burden is light
When you walk in the Spirit, you win the fight
God's word is the foundation, cut in stone
Refined in fire, impurities removed like with gold

You can never go wrong when you stick to His word
Beware of those false prophets, you must learn
They fell from grace when their hearts turned cold
You know them as sheep, but really they are wolves
That is why it is so important to come close to Him
Seek God's face by getting into His presence

Meditate in His word, by His word He is known
The First and the Last, the Ancient of Days on the throne
God and His word are one, they always agree
Submit to God's word, and the devil flees
He has no good intentions, loves only himself
Others follow him, they will burn in hell

Intercede for the sinner to send a messenger to him
Prayer is the way to do it, it's the way to start a movement
God's Spirit carries the prayer and plants it in your heart
Come to Jesus by confessing you want to make a new start
Lift the burdens and break the yoke
Praying in tongues is the master stroke

The devil can't understand it, so he's left in the dark
Prayer edifies Christ's body, you all have a part
Though not a pastor or teacher or evangelist
Everyone is an intercessor and called to assist
Time goes quickly now, even though you can't tell
There is much unfinished business, see the masses swell

Many still have not been reached
The gospel of Jesus must be preached
Think of one person you know and call his salvation in
Add to your numbers daily, intercede and pray them in
The enemy's territory is shrinking, he is losing ground
His efforts are now concentrated to tear believers down

Feeds them false information that sounds nearly true
God put His word in the Book, so the devil couldn't deceive you
Jesus is the gate, the door, and the good shepherd
There is salvation in none other, no other way to heaven
Your good works don't get you there, nor does tradition
It's about baptism of the Holy Spirit, not water baptism

Salvation and forgiveness through Jesus Christ
It's not about joining a church or family ties
You are born again only one way
Confessing Jesus as Lord are the words you must say
Keep praying, interceding, and standing in the gap
Every child of God's comes to the throne and sits in His lap

Preach the gospel, then train them up
Give them the full gospel, all God's stuff
Healing is for today, Jesus paid for it on the cross
Receive Him today and count everything else as lost
Ministering angels go forth to serve and protect
They don't preach the gospel, with people that was left

The angels lead the messenger to the sinner
The messenger imparts the word, a spark, a glimmer
The Holy Spirit convicts a sinner of the sins they do
Into the body of Christ, the Spirit baptizes you
Baptized with God's Spirit by Jesus, His Son
The evidence is seen when you pray in tongues

Be bold in your prayer and do not shy away
Send the devil packing, send him on his way
His throne shakes, and the structure rattles
Another sinner saved means he lost another battle
Intercede for the sinner and supplicate for the saints
Baby Christians need to be supported by prayers

God knocks you down with His love
The riches of the world will never be enough
His children are supernatural and recreated in His image
Pull down strongholds and cast down imaginations
Boom! Boom! Boom!
Jesus is coming soon

Fire another Volley

Inspiration: Spiritual warfare is going on all the time. Believers have authority in the name of Jesus, the presence and gifts of the Holy Spirit, and ministering angels in our God-given arsenal. Fire another volley, keep the devil on the run!

> *Scripture:* Philippians 2:9-10 (NKJV) say, "Therefore God also has highly exalted Him and given Him the name which is above every name, that at the name of Jesus every knee should bow, of those in heaven, and of those on earth, and of those under the earth,"

I search far and wide looking for the door
My eyes do not see You clearly, Lord
They cannot because they are inadequate
You are not seen, but discerned, You are Spirit
You opened a channel for us to communicate
Through Jesus, Your Son, His death was deliberate

For only by His death could death be defeated
Satan was bound, although he hasn't retreated
He has retrenched, our ignorance gives him power
Deception is his right hand in this final hour
The disasters come in waves now
Watch as he consolidates his power

The devil draws our attention away
Worldly issues lead us astray
It is deception, we busy ourselves running the course
Striving with one another for the resources
God's army moves forward all on one accord
Wave after wave, as righteousness is restored

Push the devil back and give him all you got
Authority in the name of Jesus, it's time to confront
Realize the end is near, we are in the last days
Greed and corruption, the devil's devices enter a new phase
There is one weapon you use, and it wins every time
The name of Jesus is authority, it stops Satan on a dime

Not just for your situation, get outside yourself
Call in salvations, they start in the spirit realm
Another soul saved is another soldier in the fight
Another defeat for the devil is another beam of light
Winning souls is God's desire, it's His pride and joy
Another foot on the ground is another voice to employ

The doors open for you, first in the spirit realm
Let the Holy Spirit guide you, keep Him at the helm
Everything God knows, you can't understand
His words created the heavenly expanse
You really don't want to know it all or see it all
The battles go on day and night with angels

Angels are voice-activated, they move on your word
They stop on your word, and by words they are deterred
They protect you and hedge you in
One thousand angels may fall at your left hand
Ten thousand at your right, but it shall not come near you
God's angels fight and defend, as they minister to you

When you understand the power in the Lord's name
Step out in boldness because victory has already been claimed
The power generator is Jesus, with God in heaven
The power of the Holy Spirit fueled His resurrection
Each time a sinner is saved, that power is working
Raising a dead spirit to life, to be with God eternally

Making mountains move is easy, they follow commands
They do not have a free will, God only gave that to humans
The heavens open like a curtain, He spread them wide
They didn't ask Him any questions, and they didn't strive
Every year the fish spawn in the same place
They don't turn they backs on Him, then demand to see His face

They don't worship God or offer the sacrifice of praise
He reserved that for you, only people are subject to His grace
In the spirit realm, the lines have been drawn
People's hearts are still the battleground
God won't force you to follow His word
He shows you possibilities and gives you the password

You call the shots, He loves you that much
His Spirit is hovering and keeping you in touch
He will draw you ever closer to Jesus
Live dangerously, there's so much to be done
Rebuke, exhort, and use the name of Jesus to move the devil out
Give him no place, not one little speck of ground

Don't worry about what you will eat or wear
God knows you need things, so He put them there
There for your use, just ask Him to receive
Blessings in abundance are for those who believe
You do not have, because you do not ask
Say goodbye to everything in your past

God timed everything perfectly from the beginning
And completed the works from everlasting
We are in the final stages
In the heavenlies, the battle rages
If God showed you a map, you would see the front
Fire another volley, keep the devil on the run

Battle Call

Inspiration: Praise and worship are spiritual warfare. They stop the devil and his works in their tracks. Worship is service. It requires humility, recognizing there is a God who is greater than ourselves, and that He is worthy of worship.

> *Scripture:* 2 Chronicles 20:22 (NKJV) says, "Now when they began to sing and to praise, the LORD set ambushes against the people of Ammon, Moab, and Mount Seir, who had come against Judah; and they were defeated."

Another brick wall has been put in place
God told you the way to go, it's not your way
It is contrary to your thoughts
Because you can't see the hearts
He planned it in the beginning and set the course
When you veer off, you've turned from the source

God planted you here and intends to keep you
The works you do will see you through
Continue in His word, He will never lead you astray
The works of the flesh are not spirit and hold sway
They tempt and compel, there are forces behind them
Cast them out in the name of Jesus, He gave you dominion

You are starting to see the value of worship
Give God praise and talk to Him in person
Not just to take care of your needs and wants
It's about thanksgiving and adoration
You love the things of the world and pay them attention
Seek God first, time in His presence is total fulfillment

He inhabits the praises of His people
He moves mountains, His words create upheaval
By the words you speak, the windows of heaven open
Nothing gets between God and His children
When praises flow from you to God's throne in heaven
It's a sweet perfume, His glory radiant in reflection

The devil can't stand your worship
Your adoration defeats his purpose
He shrinks into a corner when God's praises go forth
It's the love the devil doesn't like, when all are on one accord
Corporate praise and worship deflect the powers of the air
He cowers in a corner in hopelessness and despair

Jesus did it all for you, He defeated Satan in His own name
God raised Jesus from the dead after three days in the grave
Do you believe God's word? Then do it
Listen to the Holy Spirit, there aren't seven steps to it
His Spirit is omnipotent and cannot be manipulated
Jesus operates according to God's will, His timing stipulated

All things work together for good to those who love Him
You are growing in patience in following Him
God rewards those who seek Him diligently
Praise and worship are about humility
Step out of your shell and outside of yourself
Focus on Jesus and give attention to nothing else

Walk in the flow of the Holy Spirit and forget your flesh
The cares of the world and the realm of the senses
David danced before God, he let it all hang out
He was anointed and never afraid to shout it out
God blessed his life, and he accumulated much wealth
He consulted God before the temple was built

The things you want are easy to get, they're already here
See how quickly your worship brings them near
It is another phase of your relationship with the Almighty
This walk is a process and a road, so follow Jesus blindly
Be free in the Holy Spirit and shameless in your pursuit
In God's presence, the anointing comes upon you

People will think what they want, they always do
When you pray your prayers, they're not answering you
They don't butter your bread, and they don't pay your rent
God is your provider, the goods are all heaven-sent
For you, child of God, blessings in abundance await
More than you can ask or think, or even appreciate

God's words, His promises, and His love never fail
He exalted His word even above His name
If His word is no good, then He is not who He says
If God's word is no good, then He is like His creation
His word is solid, built like a brick wall
On His word, the entire universe stands or falls

I don't think you can understand it yet, the revelation
So perverted is the world system, so decrepit and tainted
Only the blood of Jesus is pure, it's spotless and sublime
One drop on the mercy seat for all time
Jesus honored God by doing His word
He said only the things that He heard

He worshipped God in spirit and in truth
Honesty and integrity are worship, they are the root
Without deep roots the plant's growth is stunted
The word goes forth in good soil, it's fruit in abundance
Hear this, child of God, the word is the key
He recompenses the time you spend, it's guaranteed

The offerings are worship, and for this He repays
All needs are met through giving, this is God's way
You can stand or sit or fall down on your knees
He sees your heart when you're connected spiritually
God knows your intents and purposes, because He sees it all
Praise and worship are the ultimate battle call

Talk to God Today

Inspiration: God has a plan for every believer and
He imparts it to us when we talk to Him.

> *Scripture:* Romans 8:15 (NKJV) says, "For you did not receive
> the spirit of bondage again to fear, but you received the Spirit
> of adoption by whom we cry out, 'Abba, Father.'"

Have you talked to God today?
Did you hear Him? What did He say?
He is our Father, He loves us so much
We feel His presence, keeping in touch

He is a Spirit, with heaven as His home
His glory came to earth, as a light it shone
That glory clothed Adam and Eve
They weren't naked, but clothed in glory

When they sinned, God's glory left the earth
It didn't return in fullness until the new birth
His glory is Jesus Christ, His anointed Son
He came to earth in the flesh, the Appointed One

He was born of the Holy Spirit, who rested upon Him
Although Jesus was tempted, He never committed sin
At Pentecost, He imparted His Spirit to the believers
Everyone can receive His Spirit, just open your receivers

When the Holy Spirit dwells inside, you come alive spiritually
He manifests His blessing to you, by faith you receive
Seek God's face, He has a plan and purpose for you
In His presence, He will show you what to pursue

God's plan is as distinct as you are, recreated in His image
His grace flows out and is never diminished
Every child of God is an important part
Part of His plan for salvation, it's about your heart

Some are apostles, some prophets, and some evangelists
Pastors, teachers, and helps ministry, it's a long list
There is much to do and so little time
Talk to Jesus, He will listen to you anytime

He has planted in each of His children a seed
Some fell by the wayside, and some on ground that was rocky
Some fell on good ground, took root, and grew
When you walk in God's path, He shows you what to do

An evangelist is not a pastor, a teacher's not a prophet
You do not choose the role you play, but the Holy Spirit
You will not reach fulfillment and never achieve
Until you follow God's instructions, after you believe

He equips those that He calls for the office He calls them to
Many do not succeed because they do what they want to do
One is not more important than the other, each has his part
God doesn't judge by the outside, but He knows your heart

When you go where God tells you, prosperity follows
In some other ministry, you will be weak and your voice hollow
It will feel like washing your feet with your socks on
Like treading water, instead of water you walk on

His burden is easy, and His yoke is light
Jesus equips you for His purpose and always gets it right
He loves to hear your voice, child of God
He never sleeps, you can talk all you want

God's blessing is wrapped up in His word
You can't live in blessing, if you've never heard
Hear His voice telling you where to step
He has placed people in line for you to help

The house built on the rock is not moved when the storm comes
Build on the sand, follow your own way, the same storm comes
The foundation is undermined, and the structure dismantled
The house not built by God cannot stand, and falls in shambles

The time you spend together is so precious
As a sweet aroma are your intercessions
This is giving of your time to help others
Do God's word, and in Him you will discover

Every hope, dream, and desire for your life fulfilled
You will never be lacking when God's vision is instilled
You take care of His stuff, and He takes care of yours
Though it takes hours, you are not doing chores

Doing God's will nourishes your spirit, it edifies and builds
It prepares you for the next level, like climbing hills
You never get to the top, because He always has more for you
As the work grows, the anointing flows, so you can do

The task is never too big, because God gave you His ability
He stretched out the heavens and created the earth and sea
He lays mountains flat and builds them up again
He is God all by Himself, He knows what and when

Confidence in your ability grows as you see what God can do
There is nothing too big, too wide, or too high, He loves you
When you step out in faith, Jesus will meet you there
His word and Spirit give life, they go everywhere

Step out and feel the joy of doing His word
Joy unspeakable and peace in your heart, feel His power
Some people are afraid to talk to God, afraid what He might ask
To go to the mission field, the hospital, or some unenviable task

When God gives you a word to do, step out
The word keeps coming until the end is brought about
Complete the word He already gave you to do
Step out and do His word, He wants to bless you

But you will never know your ministry
Until you talk to Jesus consistently
Talk to Him today, tomorrow, and every day
He loves to hear your voice in worship and praise

Come fellowship with Jesus and commune with Him
Talk to God, laugh with Him, and get in tune with Him
Give God thanksgiving and bless His Holy name
Such a sweet aroma as you talk to God today

Works

Inspiration: We busy ourselves with keeping busy. Jesus came to give us rest. In His rest, we have more perfect fellowship with God. Fellowship with Jesus leads to more rest.

> *Scripture:* Luke 8:14 (NKJV) says, "Now the ones *that* fell among thorns are those who, when they have heard, go out and are choked with cares, riches, and pleasures of life, and bring no fruit to maturity."

The flowers in the air, a fragrant smell of jasmine
The sweet aroma of praise is music in God's kingdom
You heard the mission bell, everyone to their post
Listening ears and an open heart receive the seed that's sown
God's seed bears fruit, a harvest that never fails
His word is seed, when planted in good ground, it always prevails
Weeds grow up and choke out the seed, the world has its ways
God's kingdom has life, the kingdom of eternal days

Be careful what you hear and guard your heart
Be careful how you hear, and then be ready to make a new start
Every day is a new day, every day He calls some out
The chosen are few, who are doing what He's talking about
The laughter and the dance are both expressions of joy
Means of getting the job done, with different means to employ
But it's not about the laughter, laughter is only a means
The end is brought about by the dance, which fills you with peace

Peace is what God's after for each one of His children
Get beyond the circumstances, get life in God's kingdom
His peace gives you rest, and you rest from your works
Doesn't make sense in the natural, it's one of His kingdom's perks
Rest from works and live by revelation of God's word
Each moment be led by the Holy Spirit, probably sounds absurd
His revelation is real time, it's happening now
Look at the life of Jesus, if you want to see how

Communication is fluid and fellowship continuous
Never a moment apart, and nothing is ambiguous
The spirit realm is all around, to see it takes some focus
See it in real time when you fellowship for a few moments
Talk to God from your heart, He has a listening ear
Billions of voices talking at once, each one He hears
Dreams and desires planted in you before you knew His name
Fellowship didn't just begin the day you got born again

God has been watching you since the day you were born
He loves you so much, the days apart from you leave Him torn
As He was with His Son, so He shall be with you
Jesus was firstborn from the dead, an example for you
God counted your hairs while in the womb and then made a note
His Spirit hovers over the earth today, He's searching to and fro
Searching for an open heart, one that's ready to receive
He's full of faith and power, He's resurrecting those who believe

It's a miracle every time, God yearns for the open door
Ministering salvation is like a drug for Him, He wants more
His sole ambition is that everyone be saved
It makes Him tick, opening that cold, stony grave
Lost hearts, living in deceit, that don't know any better
The dead brought back to life, it's His attention-getter
He jumps for joy and can't contain Himself, one day you'll see
Laying another stone in His building to form Christ's body

The foundation is already laid, He is Jesus, God's Son
The building rises higher as you pray in tongues
Open your heart to receive, He has an interpretation for you
Train your ear to hear, God's blessings pass through you
You are a channel and a willing vessel, He loves you so
You are workers together in God's kingdom, you must know
The little ones, just born again, are in need of a father figure
Someone in the earth realm to follow, who's pulled the trigger

The body grows together with what every joint supplies
Receiving God's word and doing His word put an end to the lies
If Habakkuk received a vision, but never wrote it down
If Jonah died inside the fish belly and never went to that town
If Abraham never left his country, there'd be no Israel today
If Jesus turned His back on God's will and refused the pain
They heard God's word and did His word and were blessed therein
Receiving from God has nothing to do with your sins

Push sins aside like He does, they have no place in His kingdom
You receive because He gives, a revelation of God's system
The keys of His kingdom open every door
He keeps giving until you can receive no more
You are limited in receiving because you limit your believing
You shouldn't be looking to the past for possibilities
Always willing and always able, Jesus is your potential
Edify yourself in the Holy Spirit, fill your bottle until it's full

Then go get another

Poems about the flesh and its war with the spirit

"Cast all your cares on Jesus, release them by faith
They tear you up inside, so why not toss them away?"

Growing Pains

"Don't give up, don't give out, and don't give in
Jesus works with you, the power is within"

Dying to Self

Growing Pains

Inspiration: We all have dreams in life. God knows our dreams because He gave them to us. His Spirit dwells inside us to help us bring those dreams to pass. He never leaves us.

> *Scripture:* 2 Corinthians 2:14 (NKJV) says, "Now thanks *be* to God who always leads us in triumph in Christ, and through us diffuses the fragrance of His knowledge in every place."

The weakness in the knees is caused by growing pains
Able to take a few steps on your own without the angst
Booming thunderstorms retreat to the pitter patter of rain
Growth in the body, fed by the food we eat, causes gain

The belt tied around your waist doesn't fit anymore
Growth in the spirit pushes open the doors
Stretched and strengthened, prodded and pushed
Press long enough, and that door opens with a whoosh

The next step doesn't get any easier, but the reward is great
You have come to the path that leads you to separate
At the crossroads, the road forks left and right
It is a critical decision, don't reason with your mind

Your spirit knows the answers, God put them there
You have to go through some things before the answered prayer
Flesh is a serious contender, gratified by short-term pleasures
Doesn't think everlasting and only uses earthly measures

Doesn't like to yield or to give way to the spirit
Has to be trained up to ignore appearances
The flesh is stupid, it's not looking to the end
It can't follow a straight path and doesn't want to bend

Flesh knows that being born again doesn't mean the war is lost
Distraction is a key element in its arsenal, with its hidden cost
You can't see tomorrow, you only believe what you see
You were created to know God and to want to believe

The soul has to be in control because the body has needs
Yield to the spirit within, you gotta practice to believe
The spirit and the flesh are both there to influence
Your soul makes the decision, its workings continuous

More and more and more and more and more
Fill up on the Holy Spirit, and watch Jesus open doors
The key to development and to a life enriched
Is personal time with Jesus, get permanently hitched

Jesus breathes on you the breath of life from above
Don't walk where the world walks, but walk in love
Your name is love, mine isn't, it's easy for You
You are the Lord's brother, which means it's easy for you too

It's a choice you make to forgive, or to love
Love isn't an emotion, it's a commitment, it's freedom
Burdens lifted and yokes removed, that's the Lord's ministry
The issues, the guilt, and the shame, give Him your inability

Cast all your cares on Jesus, release them by faith
They tear you up inside, so why not toss them away?
Faith isn't just for things, but for all the issues of life
Believing is a choice, like doing wrong or doing right

People don't want your garbage, got no time for your concerns
Got their own issues to deal with, living life as the world turns
Jesus wants all your concerns, He receives everything you've got
He burns them up with His consuming fire, a little or a lot

Keep looking forward, and then make plans to stay on the path
Clear out the issues that bind you, all the weights from the past
It's gone, it's done, and it never should have been
It hurt and changed you, you will never be the same again

You can't go around the issues, because avoidance is just delay
You must go through trouble, overcome obstacles in your way
Jesus isn't waiting in heaven, but strengthening your steps
He's either carrying you, or scooping out the mess

The world is a cruel, cold place, and not what God planned for you
Minimize its effect in your life with the things that you do
Build yourself up in His word and get to know Jesus personally
He brings things to pass that otherwise couldn't be

The dreams in your heart, you've had since you were a little girl
Don't send them away now, they came from God and not the world
They are hard-wired in your system, God put them there
To keep hope alive in you and to encourage you through despair

You will make it through when your heart is in the right place
Keep your head glued on straight, and you will finish this race
In grand style, the biggest and best that you imagined
It isn't a thought or a passing fancy, God gave you that vision

To realize dreams, there are some things you have to go through
Jesus shows you the path of peace, He burns His light inside of you
The world dumps on your head and then watches you collapse
Success is just an illusion for them, like a momentary lapse

Things they search for can't be bought for a million dollars
Seeking fulfillment in a job, your stress is building hour upon hour
Good news doesn't come in a bottle, you're just deceived
The house on the hill is nice, but it brings no eternal relief

The words God speaks are real, they were here before you
His words created the world you live in and now support it too
Before there was anything, His words came first
Created in six days, just imagine the energy burst

First there is nothing, and then there is everything
Everything spoken into reality, it's pretty amazing
The mind can't handle it, so Jesus gave you the Holy Spirit
Receive or reject Him, make the choice and define your limits

Abundance is God's will for you, but only you can make it happen
Wholeness, health, and healing, just like it is in heaven
Wrap your brain around it, embrace the idea, and make it yours
Don't worry what tomorrow will bring, just think open doors

If God created you, He had to be here before you were
He must know more than you do, He makes things sure
He is talking all the time to get His word to you
To show you the better way, open up and let Him through

Hear through your spirit and then confirm it by His word
When you become familiar with Jesus, it becomes second nature
Attune your mind to His word and His ways to get the big picture
Eliminate the confusion in your life and enjoy the adventure

No pain, no gain, that's what the world says
Wear yourself out to barely get by, that is their best
His yoke is easy, and His burden is light, His word is a lamp
Going before you in the dark places to expose their traps

It doesn't make sense, because sense comes from your head
God's word is supernatural in its origins and powerful in effect
Success is imminent because Jesus has been there before
He stands in front of you as the key to every open door

Follow Jesus like a little child, or a sheep headed for pasture
Rest and relaxation await, peace is His good pleasure
Growing pains are to be expected as you bring the flesh in line
Get your head in tune with the Holy Spirit, and you will be just fine

Press Through

Inspiration: Believers must press through the flesh and
the world's system of doing things to get all of God. If we
stand still and stay in place, really we are falling behind,
because the world keeps moving forward all around us.

> *Scripture:* Philippians 3:14 (NKJV) says, "I press toward the
> goal for the prize of the upward call of God in Christ Jesus."

If you do not step forward, you will be left behind
It's the salvation principle that works in the spirit, not the mind
If you compromise too many times, it becomes normal
God has placed a calling on your life that is irrevocable

Step up, step in, step out, and into the plan He has for you
Nature's calling you, it's the flesh trying to press through
Press back, push it back, and keep it under, you are in control
Let your spirit take charge by overcoming the soul

Your life in Jesus is lived as His life in you
You're going to another realm, press through
Healing is in God's wings, it belongs to you, His gift
In His presence is abundant life, everything you wished

Never mind the world or the things therein, they are oppressing
They knock you down, drag you around, and block God's blessings
His word is the revelation and takes you to a different level
The level of the spirit realm, the place where He dwells

You used to be there with Him, that's why your flesh cries out
Struggles as though still in the dark, still thirsty in a drought
Don't walk in the dark, Jesus bought you back from there
Redemption in Jesus' blood, deliverance from worldly despair

His method is life, His motive is love, and His way is truth
Just words to the world, He bought you back because He values you
Dwell with Jesus in a heavenly dwelling place
You once were in the garden, communicating face-to-face

A home that you cannot now see, but soon He will open your eyes
The eyes of the whole world watch as the dead in the graves arise
With a shout and a trumpet blast, His Son, Jesus is coming soon
Never doubt His word, He brings it to pass, He cannot lie to you

God has no interest in compromise, He brings only victory
He doesn't negotiate with losers, His word is reality
It is His bond, His solemn vow, and His guarantee to you
He is no respecter of persons, He gave His word for each one of you

Work the system, and then watch the system work you over
It was designed by the devil to fail, he's the indecent proposer
He is real, he is spirit, and he brings only destruction
Death and loss, lack and sorrow, total obstruction

He presses your mind and works through your flesh
Works as you yield to him, and together you make a mess
Salvation is the gift Jesus gave you, a transaction, not a process
Choose your words carefully, they have power for success

Jesus works through you in the earth, He gave you dominion
He will not override your will, no matter His opinion
You hold God to His words, and He holds you to yours
They ignite the progression of His plan, which is spotless and pure

Truth is what you believe it to be, but only God is reality
Your words speak things into existence, for worse or for victory
Inhabit His presence as the equal of Jesus, in all righteousness
God's kingdom and glory are there, so continue to press

In might and dominion and authority and power
Take back what was stolen from you to build that strong tower
Start with a firm foundation, His word never fails
Tested and tried, His righteousness always prevails

You are a king and a priest, a prophet full of dreams
Visions come from God's presence, flowing rivers and streams
Nothing is too hard for Jesus, He lives inside you, so press through
Focus, concentrate, and let Him do what He came here to do

To understand the end, you must understand the beginning
God brings it to pass just as He planned, pruning and trimming
He completed the works when He laid the foundation
People confessing the name of Jesus, nation by nation

You can't do it on your own, in honesty, you never could
The Holy Spirit in you completes the works, bringing about good
He dwells in you and operates through you, doing the works
Press into Him, and then He flows out of you, not in fits and spurts

A continuous flow, the power is there, the mantle has been passed
Jesus ministers from heaven, His Spirit hovering 'til the last
Do the works Jesus did, and do greater even than these
His Spirit lives in you, so press through, in this He is well-pleased

Issues

Inspiration: I started writing this poem in September 2016. I was frustrated, so I wrote down my frustration. The poem sat there for a couple months. I wrote a couple more lines. It sat again. Then I wrote 1 more line. And it sat again. I picked it up on March 2, 2017 and the Holy Spirit completed the final 2 pages in one sitting, starting with "Jesus never said He'd run for you." It was agonizing to write the first page. But the last 2 pages came as fast as I could write them down. It took 6 months to finish. Ah, patience. The Holy Spirit told me exactly what I needed to hear.

Scripture: 1 Corinthians 3:9 (NKJV) says, "For we are God's fellow workers; you are God's field, *you are* God's building."

Wasting away
What can I say?
Can't do what I want
Don't really know what to want

Did what You told me to do
Would I have done differently, if I knew?
A look into the future, if only I'd seen
If I could've chosen, would I have gone blindly?

I heard Your voice, I knew what You said
But really I had no clue what it meant
I thought I faced all the rejection I was gonna face
I thought making that decision meant I'd finish the race

I thought it could never get any worse
Was I getting the promise or living the curse?
Is being lost different than being empty?
Having no vision, not sure I want to see

Never had a dream or an overwhelming desire
Nothing seems to matter, just gotta climb to get higher
No one to rely on, and no one relying on me
Seems like freedom, but I don't really feel free

There is a right way and a wrong way
Do what you're gonna do, say what you're gonna say
Getting up feels just like falling down
That spinning wheel keeps spinning around

Satisfy yourself and let everybody down
Looking for a smile, but feeling like a frown
Then comes Jesus, tried and true
He keeps calling, He's still in hot pursuit

You stumble and fall, you messed up again
He's always there by your side with a stretched out hand
His vision and His plan work together for good
The difficult part is for it to be understood

You talked through a donkey, but can you really use me?
I messed up again, but You said You'd never refuse me
Aches and pains and groanings erupt
Can't see tomorrow, and today is corrupt

Never failing and never ending, His love comes by grace
Get to the finish line, so I can't start the race
Jesus never said He'd run for you, you have to choose
He said He'd run with you, and that together you'd never lose

Coworkers together, there's gonna be a fight
The Bible said so, and His word is always right
You got stuck on yourself and dug a hole deep
You pulled the dirt in around you and built walls steep

You gotta climb out step-by-step
Jesus could pull you up quickly, but you'd only fall back again
You're comfortable and lazy, waiting on answers from Him
Jesus never sleeps, He's working for you, He's comforting

He cries out to you, and you cry out to Him
He hears you, but you don't hear Him
There's a communication problem alright, and it starts with you
You pay attention to your flesh when it tells you what to do

Flesh knows what you like
It gives you what you like
Jesus gives you what you need
You need to build your capacity

There's more to do and so little time
You sit around and cry out 'where's mine?'
It's where you left it
Are you gonna go back and get it?

Or move forward with Jesus, step into tomorrow?
He told you how, and He told you when, you just gotta follow
Follow Jesus, the narrow path
The gate opens wide, but stay off the grass

Come toward Jesus, closer to Him, and pray your way through
Prayer connects you with Him, He is longing to hear you
To connect with you, to build you up, and to inspire
Crooked places made straight, you just gotta inquire

God can go on without you, but it wouldn't be the same
Gifts He's worked through you, things you do in Jesus' name
It is command and control and standing in the gap
He leaves the door wide open, so that everybody has a chance

Balaam didn't see the Angel, but heard the donkey speak
That is God's power in action, as deep calls unto deep
You wanna see a sign, so does everybody else
Jesus works through you, not through fairies and elves

If you give up, He doesn't stand a chance
You've only just begun your Godly romance
It doesn't work without you
And Jesus wouldn't want it to

God put all His power in you
He gave you His love to help you through
You've got issues, Jesus is the only person who doesn't
He achieved perfection for you, He's the death that later wasn't

Jesus defeated death, guilt, and shame
He took all your sins, and still they defamed His name
They plucked out His beard and beat Him with rods
While He hung on that cross, they taunted Him: what a God!

It's ok, He did it for you, He knew in the end
Jesus knew the plan from the beginning, He'd live again
He's alive now, He's been glorified
He's seated in heaven, His post soarified

He's still ministering as your Mediator and High Priest
He's interceding for you from the last to the least
Jesus hasn't forgotten you or your struggles
He will lead you through them, whatever befuddles

One nail went through His right hand, one through the left
Don't ever deny it and don't ever forget
Jesus bled for you, He died for you, and took it all
He died once for all, He always takes your call

If you're feeling down, it's not the Lord's fault
Turn on some lights, and add a little salt
Jesus never leaves you nor forsakes you, He stands His post
Jesus loves you more and more, He loves you most

Flesh Colored Glasses

Inspiration: Discrimination isn't just an American problem, or a 'white' people's problem. It happens all over the world. God created us of one blood. We all descended from Adam. It is the Spirit dwelling inside us that binds us together.

> *Scripture:* Galatians 3:28 (NKJV) says, "There is neither Jew nor Greek, there is neither slave nor free, there is neither male nor female; for you are all one in Christ Jesus."

With you or without you, God's word is the same
The highest and the best to magnify His name
Higher than the highest high
Your spirit laughs, and your brain wonders why
Glorify Jesus and exalt Him, exceedingly, abundantly
Open your eyes to the spirit realm, so you can see

Never mind the flesh or the works thereof
In the beginning, the two were together as one
The flesh with the spirit, created in love
Created by God, to always dwell with Him above
Long lasting and life-changing, His word has power
Hails in the second coming, it's coming in a few hours

God's word impales your heart and bursts the bonds that bind
A more important life event you will never find
The world has its ways, its rhythms, and its rhymes
Like mixing oil and water, as you skim along with time
Not leading or guiding, don't try to mix with the world
The world doesn't work, you're just jumping hurdles

It's all about you and using the power to intimidate
The power of the gospel of Jesus, the power that gets people saved
Do not abuse it or use it to advance your cause
Manipulation is witchcraft, like magnifying flaws
You are the color God made you, for some it is a challenge
A stumbling block and a hindrance, it causes imbalance

In all things, you are more than a conqueror
All nations were created of one blood, not three or four
Beautiful in God's eyes, all created in Their image
Made of the dust of the earth as inspired flesh
Black, white, brown, and yellow, or even if blue or green
At the new birth you inherit God's Spirit, you're clothed in glory

He doesn't judge you by your flesh, but by the life within
Color, culture, and wealth are things that have no bearing
There are differences for sure, explained by the genes
But all people came from one place, a divergence of one seed
Looking through flesh-colored glasses, you are so easily deceived
The flesh is the veil, that even now is in retreat

Walking around with burdens from the world, heavy weights
Can't understand why the frustration never seems to go away
He is a burden remover and a yoke smasher, Jesus the Christ
Refreshing and restoration are in His words of life
God is Spirit, His fruit doesn't grow on a tree
It grows in your hearts, it's the incorruptible Seed

Receive Jesus into the boat, and resolution comes immediately
Apply the word to your circumstances, and the storms cease
Apply the word to your flesh and listen to what you hear
Jesus leads you with His word to make your direction clear
Your flesh is a barrier He won't cross, His integrity is on the line
God brings His word to pass and always at the perfect time

He is talking all the time, if your spirit is open to receive
His word clears away the clutter and then clears your path to Jesus
That undulating snake, that twisted serpent of old
Sometimes a pit viper or a constrictor with a strangle hold
Little by little, Satan chips away at God's word to create doubt
Sometimes a gentle prod and sometimes an unbearable shout

'The deceiver' because he copies God's ways, and with success
But peace never comes, you are never able to enter God's rest
The devil operates through your flesh and plays with your mind
If you don't know the truth, then you are drawn to story time
He is a master of disguises and seemingly credible
When you follow him, a fall is inevitable

Spend time with Jesus, get to know Him, lay the foundation deep
Build on the rock of His word that always brings consistency
No more up's and down's and no more confusing mess
His word is a sure-footing, you don't have to second guess
You don't have to spend all day going back and forth
Listen for His voice, do what He says, and emerge as victors

God leads by your spirit, so shut down the voice in your head
He speaks through your spirit, but the other voice leads to death
The road to poverty is paved with excuses
When they are removed, you see only solutions
The true leader takes you in a new direction and lights a new path
Makes the crooked places straight, isn't looking for the last laugh

God made each one of you unique, each has a special place
With a special purpose, but my, you are a peculiar race
You are not from this world, recreated in word and power
Wait 'til you see what you look like in that final hour
Love one another as Jesus loves you, a great command
Hurdle the stumbling blocks of the flesh and get with God's plan

Pruning the Vine

Inspiration: This poem talks about stepping away from a friendship in order to stay where God wants you to be.

> *Scripture:* John 15:6 (NKJV) says, "If anyone does not abide in Me, he is cast out as a branch and is withered; and they gather them and throw *them* into the fire, and they are burned."

You can cry if you want to
The tears come because you didn't do what you were supposed to do
You did not seek God or His authority
You cannot follow the ways of society

You have been called to God for His purpose
You can no longer skim along the surface
Half of your time in the world and half out
Piano strings are tightened to perfect the sound

Like a piano, you are being fine-tuned
God trims and cuts away impediments when He prunes
Every branch on the vine is treated the same way
Cutting off the impotent strengthens what remains

The pain you feel in your heart for a lost friend
Will turn to joy when the new sprouts begin
The world has their way of doing things, not by God's design
There is a great gulf fixed between them, you cannot cross the line

He has told you some things that He has for you
Some are easier than others, just be sure to follow through
You can go around this mountain as many times as you want
You took a bold step today, it was best to confront

Like burning all the bridges behind you
There is nothing there for you to go back to
You are closer to where God wants you to be
In the place where you see only reality

Behold the Image of Jesus

Inspiration: Look to the word when you have difficulties. Jesus knows you inside and out and knows the direction you need.

> *Scripture:* John 10:3 (NKJV) says, "To him the doorkeeper opens, and the sheep hear his voice; and he calls his own sheep by name and leads them out."

When the only thing you're hanging on to starts slipping away
The sun comes up, but you're not looking for another day
Can't see to the left and don't know what's right
Take that step forward, oh, maybe you just might

Jesus knows how you feel, He's been there and done that
So easy to contemplate, there's no need to be hesitant
It's new and different, and up ahead is the narrow gate
His word drenches you, its purpose is to satiate

Take a taste, take a bite, and swallow it whole
You can take tiny bites, but that goes so slow
God hears you when you cry, He gave you that voice
He asked you to follow Jesus, but gave you the choice

You weren't forced, He gave you options
It's a different path, God understands if you are cautious
He called you and blessed you, and you are anointed
He gave you power when you were appointed

You're outta control, with pride like a billy goat
He lowered the draw bridge, and you crossed the moat
Into the castle, with its dungeon laid bare
You walked into the midst of the devil's lair

Push 'em over, knock 'em down, and watch them crawl
Invading their territory is crashing a monster's ball
We overtake and overcome, we're fellow workers with Him
If it doesn't work the first time, just try it again

God understands it's hard, He told you once upon a time
If it were easy everyone'd do it, you left in your prime
The quirks, the quivers, and the quiet solitude
It's where God can reach you and nudge you with the truth

The truth is what's real, it's behind the open door
The door that never closes, it's open forevermore
Open to those who listen and to those who learn
To those who answer, like the prow to the stern

You want to see the step before you place your foot
But that's not God's way, He breaks it down, it's all good
He made it easy, so simple, step-by-step
Heaven's the open door, the believers are a tiny speck

Put many specks together to fill in the dot
Clothes match better when cut from the same cloth
Into the mirror we go, beholding the Lord's image
Where the veil is taken away, and so are the limits

Reality

Inspiration: In the New Testament, one of the definitions of "truth" is "reality." Things in the spirit realm are more real than things in the natural. Moving out on the word that we hear is acting in faith. Don't be discouraged in doing what the Lord told you to do. Completely open yourself to God.

> *Scripture:* Philippians 1:6 (NKJV) says, "being confident of this very thing, that He who has begun a good work in you will complete *it* until the day of Jesus Christ;"

He is the God of source and supply
Drink of Him to live and not die
The food you eat feeds you spiritually
In God's word is everything you will ever need

Every soul yielded is the thing He craves
Jesus offers you eternal life and an open grave
Mistakes are made, sometimes you stumble
He lifts you up, fills you up, and raises you to rumble

Your words bring death, or they bring life
In God's presence is peace only, not strife
The path you are on is not easy for now
Jesus will lead you and show you how

Compromises cannot continue
His kingdom has a narrow path, He needs you
Step up, step out, and step on the devil's throat
Encourage those who follow, step into the overflow

Some get so close but never feel God's presence
Complete release is the only way, let go of your senses
Sever your ties with the world and let them go
If you spend time to nurture them, they will grow

Emotions can add value, but can also take you away from Jesus
Happenstance or circumstance have no place in His reality
You know what you know, and do what you know to do
There is not much longer until this thing is through

God planned it all in the beginning, soon you will see
He is not a stab in the dark, He is where He'll always be
Dabble here and dabble there, but focus on the Almighty
When you come closer to Jesus, you come closer to reality

Dying to Self

Inspiration: The flesh is independent of the spirit. It will
lead you, until and unless you bring it under subjection
to your born-again spirit. God gives us the Holy Spirit
and His word to help us overcome the ways of the flesh.
If you are looking for direction in life, look to Jesus.

> *Scripture:* Romans 8:5 (NKJV) says, "For those who live
> according to the flesh set their minds on the things of the
> flesh, but those *who live* according to the Spirit, the things of
> the Spirit."

I don't really know where I'm going to
The only thing that matters is following You
Take up the cross and follow Jesus
He took all the sin of the world to give us freedom

It's not an easy place to get to, this dying to self
Just look at Jesus and don't see nothing else
The flesh is the weakness, it has its own voice
Deprive it for a while and don't listen to all the noise

Flesh can't come and go just when it pleases
The mind is really in control, oh, how it teases
Line upon line, precept upon precept
Evil company corrupts good habits

Evil doesn't mean bad, but without God
Having no reverence and following your own thoughts
Doesn't matter if you think it's good
Don't think it's good, just because people approve

The anointing has lifted, now what do you do?
If you were Elijah, you would run too
He wasn't afraid, he was empty
A horse without a rider, a sail without a sea

Here and there and back and forth
Round and round you go, looking for the door
With intercessory prayer, the edifice rises
Praying in tongues is doing faith exercises

Do it because you want to, or even if you don't
There are answers that come from heaven's throne
If God didn't mean it, He wouldn't have said it
Go boldly forth and don't be hesitant

You can't go forth, because you can't see it
It's right on top of you, you only gotta believe it
Can't get there by sittin' around watching tv
Doesn't matter what you know or how you feel

Matters what you hear and what you see
Only really matters if you see what God sees
He gave you the seed, all you gotta do is plant it
Sow it into good ground, but don't abandon it

Tilled and weeded and watered and fed
Sunlight shines from above and gives nourishment
You can predict the harvest but never know
So many distractions can disrupt the growth

Don't see the process, but know it works
The harvest comes from water, seed, and dirt
You still don't know where you're going, but Jesus does
The seed was planted inside when you washed in His blood

God's thoughts and plans for you are all good
You would try to make it on your own, if you thought you could
Tomorrow always comes and never misses a beat
Put your genius aside, just let your mind have a seat

God's timing is perfect, and His love is true
After Jesus died, how could He leave you?
He went through a lot to get through to you
He's not complaining, He's just reminding you

Stop reasoning with your mind, it doesn't make sense
Never lose your hope, but stand firm with confidence
You want the prize, but haven't finished the race
You want some power, but don't know God's ways

You think you got it all down, but you don't
You say the world ends today, but it won't
False prophets abound, just big fat liars
Deceiving the masses and passing out flyers

You tune in, when you should be tuning out
God said these things would come, do you believe Him now?
You are in control because He put you there
The power is in you, just be aware

Fellow workers with Jesus, true laborers, are few
So many in need, there are billions in the queue
Don't give up, don't give out, and don't give in
Jesus works with you, the power is within

Flows through you like electricity through the lines
God is the power source, the One who supplies
Unlimited power, greater than the hydrogen bomb
The power that moves mountains and makes seas calm

Keep looking back in time, further and further you go
Jesus is there at the beginning, and one day everyone will know
One day He'll open the books to tell the whole story
The way it is, was, and will be, it started with God's glory

So keep walking forward in the way you know
Until you hear the voice of Jesus again, then you will know
Sound, true, perfect, and correct
Dying to self is how you progress

Poems With Miscellaneous Themes

"When you hit the wall and tried everything to succeed
Cry out to Jesus, grace and more grace is what you need"

Grace

"Believers are not just old sinners saved by grace
At God's right hand in heaven is your rightful place"

Why Did Grandpa Die Poor?

When I was Nine

Inspiration: Some of us could say that there are things in our lives that we would like to forget, things that we wish had never happened. If we let the world's opinion guide us, we will still be in the same place 20, 30, or even 40 years later, with our backs still to the wall. Thank God that there are only 2 qualifiers to be delivered from that situation: 1) confess Jesus Christ as our Lord and Savior and 2) believe in our heart that God raised Him from the dead. No matter where you come from, or how bad you think your past was, God remits your sins when you confess Jesus as Lord and Savior. He cleanses away the hurt and shame. Glory!

> *Scripture:* Matthew 19:14 (NKJV) says, "But Jesus said, 'Let the little children come to Me, and do not forbid them; for of such is the kingdom of heaven.'"

When I was nine

I told You that if this was all there was for me
If this was all You had for me
That I didn't want it, please kill me now
I had gotten to the place where I couldn't see how
How I would ever be happy
How anyone could ever love me

But a voice came just then and said
The most important words that I will never forget
'This is not all I have for you
This is not what your life will be about'
When the challenge comes, God shows us the way out

So many times in my life
I just wanted to curl up and die
But this hope inside me never left
Those words when I was nine I will never forget
Other people looked at me and thought I was proud
Even called me 'Miss high and mighty' out loud
Trying to shame me and pull me back down
To the place of despair where I couldn't get out

Your Spirit in me kept me strong
Though I didn't know then where it came from
I didn't know You were protecting me
Shielding me and urging me to believe

Many years of my life I passed with ups and downs
More downs than ups, when I think back now
The alcohol and games could never satisfy me
That voice said there was something else, had it passed by me?
Had I gone so far away from God?
Maybe He had given up on me, I thought
I would have if I were Him
The things I'd done, how could they be forgiven?

I left my church because I never learned anything
Maybe the ABC's of hypocrisy, but nothing
Nothing that changed my life or made the guilt disappear
The shame of what I'd been through brought fear
And nightmares and feelings of guilt and doubt
I was a prisoner of that past, I was bound
Where was that voice I heard when I was nine?
Would He still pay attention to me after all this time?

I spoke to God from my heart
I wanted to make a new start
I wanted to go a church to get closer to Him
A few days later, a knock on the door, and my answer walked in

Some of us go through life, and we blame God
For the bad things done to us, and why not?
He's in charge, isn't He? He's the one who made it all
In six days the Book of Genesis says, as I recall
He's the one who lets people do the things they do
If God's in charge, who can we turn to?
He doesn't want us to be rich, because poverty is a sign of humility
He wants us to be sick, if we suffer for Him, then He gets the glory
He's in charge, isn't He?
He's the one putting it all on me
And I'm supposed to ask Him to heal me?

Doesn't make sense, it's just a bunch of confusion
Dad died young, from a long-term condition
The Lord finally took him and ended his suffering
What a merciful God, who finally put him out of his misery
That's what I was told by the church, and I believed them
Who was I to question a priest? Seemed like the reason
He was reading the Bible for 40 years, or so I thought
But my Bible says God delivers us out

His Son died on a tree
To take sickness away from me
If God's putting it on and taking it off
That's confusion, and that's why people scoff
Scoff at Christianity today, why believe in God?
A god who puts sickness on me, who tries to take my life?
If God's in charge of the earth, what does heaven look like?

Then I went to a church where they taught me the word
God doesn't bring the problem but gives strength to endure
He uses every trial and tribulation and test
To build in me the spirit He needs to clean up the mess
The mess left by years of ignorance and bad teaching
For those who endure the challenge, God is always reaching
To put them on the front battle lines
They have already been tested by fire

Never forget the voice that spoke to you
Who told you the things He had for you
He will strengthen you and guide you through
He will never lie, and His word is always true
That when He formed me, He had a plan
A purpose in creating me, I just had to stand
Stand long enough to get through the devil's fiery darts
I made it through life's difficult start
I was no afterthought to God, I was no accident
I am God's own child, not just some honorable mention
I am one of the branches of the vine
I was made for this moment in time

He revealed that to me when I was nine

Grace

Inspiration: Grace is God's undeserved, or unmerited, favor extended to believers through Jesus Christ. Grace is also power, God's energy. And it's a free gift! It's free!

Scripture: James 4:6 (AMP) says, "But He gives us more and more grace (power of the Holy Spirit, to meet this evil tendency and all others fully). That is why He says, God sets Himself against the proud and haughty, but gives grace [continually] to the lowly (those who are humble enough to receive it)."

Grace is God's favor, you didn't deserve it
Confession of Jesus Christ is how you earn it
God gives you grace, so you can be saved
It is the power of the new birth, received through faith
Grace is the Holy Spirit, who gives you power
It comes in His timing, in the exact hour
Grace is God's ability and is never wasted
Sends manna pouring from heavenly places

Grace is God's anointing, upon you it rests
It provides endurance to alleviate stress
Grace is supernatural and unconditional love
When God calls you to ministry, He anoints you from above
Fulfill His calling and do the works
Grace is His Spirit who conducts the search
To and fro throughout the earth, He imparts
This new life is eternal, by grace the flow starts

Grace rests upon the believer through Jesus, God's Son
The power that fueled His life and resurrection
Grace is God's compassion in demonstration
His love and mercy beyond imagination
Grace gives you the power to overcome
You have the victory in every situation
Your faith by itself gets nothing done
Grace answers prayers in the name of Jesus

When you confess Jesus as Savior and Lord
Grace pours from heaven, more upon more
The world brings you trials, tribulations, and tests
Grace in you leads you through the mess
When confusion hits you, you've stepped into the flesh
Grace can restore, heal, and repair all the damage
Heals the sick of each and every disease
It's the storehouse that supplies your needs

Grace is God's anointing to destroy the yoke
That opens your eyes to understand the hope
Grace shows the power that raised Jesus from the dead
And imparts the fruit of the spirit when you're born again
Your words speak it and then grace brings it to pass
Grace opens the heavenly gates to the righteous
It is forgiveness of all sins past, present, and future
Imparts His word and builds you up like a booster

God's grace is abundance, the blessing went forth
When He spoke to Adam, grace was the source
It is His grace that led Abram from his home
Grace that gave Solomon the wisdom
That led Jehoshaphat into battle
The choir in front, their nerves not rattled
Grace covered Adam and Eve in the garden
And gave the Israelites the Ten Commandments

The blood of goats and calves never did satisfy Him
The blood of Jesus covered the mercy seat in heaven
Grace accepted His death for all humankind
And sent the Holy Spirit to you, you're forever entwined
His grace forgives you and overcomes every sin
Even the sins of the sinners have been forgiven
When you hit the wall and tried everything to succeed
Cry out to Jesus, grace and more grace is what you need

Grace is His love and is never diminished
It's the power you need, the works are not yet finished
Grace is for the humble and those willing to receive
It's the talent Jesus placed in those who believe
It's the opposite of works, to the spirit we yield
Grace is His covering and acts as a shield
It's the prompt from the Spirit to give
When your flesh is weak, God's grace is sufficient

Grace through faith is what moves mountains
Faith is the channel that receives, no doubtin'
Grace flows like oil through the lamp
It's the rod in your back that stiffens you to stand
Grace is God's love without partiality
Extended to everyone, just receive
God has mountains of grace stored up for you
Call on Jesus, and His grace answers you

Commercial Love

Inspiration: One purpose of the church is to help believers grow in the things of God. Another is to reach out to sinners. There are a lot of different churches, each with a different assignment. Some fulfill their assignment, and some don't.

> *Scripture:* John 21:15 (NKJV) says, "So when they had eaten breakfast, Jesus said to Simon Peter, 'Simon, *son* of Jonah, do you love Me more than these?' He said to Him, 'Yes, Lord; You know that I love You.' He said to him, 'Feed My lambs.'"

You can bend it and twist it, any way you like
Don't go too deep, just flash 'em that celebrity smile
They love you, and some will even believe you for a while
You move on and leave them cold, and then they realize

Life is hard, and love is real
You can fake 'em both for the price of a happy meal
Doesn't matter where the heart is, just make your appeal
They genuflect and smile, and then they close the deal

Commercial love is when you do for you
When it's convenient, it can be profitable too
The glitter and glitz, they put on a good show
They work behind the cameras, making it grow

The wardrobe department, makeup, and hair
Just like Hollywood, nobody's listening, they only stare
The flesh has priority, its goal is to beguile
Not what God wanted in a Christian's profile

Curses without cause do not alight
The thief comes in the darkness, lurking in the night
He isn't fooled, but rather intrigued
The mystery is solved, success in deceit

Never mind the word or the pitter patter
Centuries to build but only seconds to shatter
Clitter clatter on the roof, inside the titter tatter
So much noise, can't tell what's the matter

God can't rejoice or condone this mess
The medals of the battles assembled on His chest
Hear this, child of God, and hear Him good
He would come down here and fix it if He could

But He can't, He won't, that's why He sent you
No time to run now, there's still so much to do
He can't do it without you, He made each child distinct
Don't just dip your toe in the water, jump in and take a drink

The storm on the horizon is blowing in fast
Your eyes see, your mouth speaks, and then it blows past
Powerful words move mountains, it starts with power
Empty words move the crowd, they're transfixed for hours

Forms, but no substance, and clouds without water
Dry river beds, valley of dry bones, and modern marauders
No life and no power, words spoken only to impress
And they do for a while, they make a big commercial mess

Put up the tent and raise the big top
The century's finest show has arrived on the spot
Can't hear and can't see, but sound good and look better
Don't receive the Spirit, only understand the letter

It's about money, we all know that
Not how God thinks, thinking like that
The world runs on money, it's not about love
A good show, a show stopper, it's commercial love

Justify it, sort it out, and grab at it while you can
Not long now and you'll see the second coming of Man
It's what we wait for, believe in, and hope for
Commercial love can be bought, seems every year it costs more

Leaves you empty inside, keep kicking the can down the street
Searching for hope and getting the milk, but where's the meat?
When it finally hits you, there's no gas left
All your energy's gone, their veil has been rent

Trust us, you say, because we were sent
Don't bother with important things, like getting born again
The cologne smells nice, and the makeup is perfect
Commercial love, celebrity smile, your game is checked

Why Did Grandpa Die Poor?

Inspiration: A friend of mine, a longtime Christian, asked me 'if God is so good, why did my Grandpa die poor?' So I took the question to the Lord, and He gave me this poem. We tend to judge people by what we see on the outside, but God judges our hearts.

Scripture: 2 Corinthians 5:17 (NKJV) says, "Therefore, if anyone *is* in Christ, *he is* a new creation; old things have passed away; behold, all things have become new."

Why did your grandfather die poor?
He served in church nearly every day, you expected more
What a great man of God, he was loyal and true
He was committed and dedicated, everyone knew

God rewards you for the things you do
He also sees that which is hidden from view
He searches the minds and hearts
In the beginning, He formed your inner parts

Some say it's not right to question God
There is a time and a place to do it, and why not?
He gave human beings a place a little lower than Him
His Spirit teaches you things to bring understanding

God is not to blame for your poverty or lack
He gave the Bible to navigate like a road map
He tells you to ask anything in the Lord's name
And He will give it to you, He will not be put to shame

You have a responsibility to walk in love
Faith and confessions are good, but not enough
If you love the brethren, you know you have eternal life
Prayers don't go anywhere if you're are always in strife

Unforgiveness is the fly in the ointment
It spoils the love walk and brings only disappointment
Love your neighbor as yourself is the new commandment
Love Jesus with your whole heart, He is worthy of reverence

You know Jesus is perfect, He is never wrong
If something is lacking in your life, it's not His fault
He sent His word to show you the way
It's up to you to learn it, what does it say?

Meditate on the word both day and night
Do what the word says, because the word is always right
Can anyone say why one is poor and another rich?
Only God knows, He judges the spirits

You see the outside, what is perceived by the senses
God formed you in the womb, He knows your intentions
Ignorance of the word destroys His children
Disobedience of His word keeps you imprisoned

You cannot enjoy the abundant life without knowledge
You cannot enjoy healing, if you think God keeps you in bondage
If you do not understand that in Christ you are righteous
You will run from Him and not seek forgiveness

Believers are not just old sinners saved by grace
At God's right hand in heaven is your rightful place
You inherited Abraham's blessings
Because Jesus sacrificed Himself for all of us

'Hypocrites' is what Jesus called the scribes and Pharisees
They were concerned with keeping the outside of the vessel clean
They sat in the front row of the synagogue
They prayed loudly, so others would notice and talk

They criticized others for not following the law
Even they couldn't keep it, breaking one law made you guilty of all
They criticized Jesus for calling God His father
They didn't understand, they were servants under the law

Once you are saved by grace through faith
There is no condemnation the rest of your days
You are a new creation, old things become new
The Holy Spirit takes up residence inside of you

I don't know why grandpa died poor
But if he was saved, don't worry, he lives forevermore
You can walk around during this life in defeat
Or get into God's word and walk in victory

Liberty Costs

Inspiration: Financially supporting the gospel is
part of a Christian's assignment. The Bible needs
to be taught and teaching costs money.

> *Scripture:* 1 Corinthians 9:14 (NKJV) says, "Even so the Lord
> has commanded that those who preach the gospel should live
> from the gospel."

Life in Jesus is a life in liberty
Liberty in Christ based on what you believe
He came to give us life and life more abundantly
He's God, so He knows what we need

Blessings accrue to you by sowing seed
God never desired His people to live in poverty
So many people miss it by just waiting on God
We have our part to play, first we need to be taught

Life in God is not some big lottery in the sky
Don't wait for abundance in the sweet bye-and-bye
The Bible talks about money more than heaven
He knows you need money to keep the gospel spreading

Abundance is your witness to Jesus
His word is true, if He says it, you can believe it
The Bibles, the churches, and pews all cost money
When the preacher asks for money, he's not being funny

Tithing is to support the needs of the local church
And to help spread the gospel to the ends of the earth
We don't travel by donkey anymore
Fuel costs money, seems every day it costs more

Money for buildings or stadiums in which to preach
Airplanes carry the pastors to where they teach
Churches have employees who all need to be paid
Families to feed and bills to pay, even after they are saved

Everyone welcomes crusaders to the mission field
People are blessed by their words, when God is revealed
But ask for a donation to pay the bills, and people squawk
Money doesn't fall from the sky, wouldn't that be a shock?

If you don't want to give to support the gospel, that's fine
Others will tire of paying your way in time
Missionaries have been sent for hundreds of years
You follow traditions instead of opening your ears

The Bible says he who preaches the gospel, by it he should live
Income and sustenance come from the money you give
God doesn't want to see His pastor going door-to-door
Begging and pleading for funds to feed the poor

By poor he means himself, when he can't feed his family
You look to someone else to give him something to eat
He serves God's people by preaching His word
Teaching His word, so the Holy Spirit is conferred

Bill Gates makes billions selling software to the masses
If he were in town, everyone would attend his classes
To see how he did it, and where all the money came from
From the computer industry he serves, that's how it is done

The Bible tells you to pay tithes and give offerings
Tithes are required, by the Spirit offerings are given
Pastors are appointed by God, not beggars in the street
The local church should be supporting their need

God said to give, and it shall be given back to you
He returns what you give in the measure you use
Giving is not about money but obedience
You read the word and hear His voice, these are ingredients

The other part of the recipe is to do the word
The Rhema and Logos are required
Without money, there is no television
Without money, there is no investment

God's word supplies everything you need
You want money, then start sowing seed
His word is universal and works everywhere on the planet
All are saved the same way, equal opportunity, God planned it

Liberty comes from seeking God as your source
He is the vine, and you are the branches, of course
The branch grows from the life of the vine
Believers can do nothing without the vine's life

The branch grows by feeding on Him faithfully
His word is the source to supply you bountifully
Quit looking to people, to the left or to the right
People are created beings, and not the source of the light

People teach and you learn that way, it's true
Always check in God's word, let no one deceive you
Many deceivers have gone into the world in these last days
Disguised as angels of light, carefully study their ways

If God's word doesn't say it, then it didn't come from Him
His testimony is manipulated by the false prophet
Test the spirits, Jesus came in the flesh and is Lord
If they can't confess that, then they are to be ignored

God's word is to be rightly divided
Love, peace, and joy eternally provided
Love does no wrong to a neighbor, and love forgives
Love prays for an enemy, and love gives

Follow God's example, He loved and gave His Son
God gave Jesus for sinners through salvation
It is easy to love one who loves you
It is easy to bless one who blesses you

Pray for those who scorn and revile you
Those who persecute, curse, and lie about you
When Jesus came to the world, no one was saved
They were aliens from God, and hell was their grave

By giving Jesus, God stretched out His hand
To those who for centuries turned their backs
Jesus knew no sin, yet bore the world's sin
Even for those who didn't know Him

Sinners sin because that is what they are
You were once there, but have come so far
They need the gospel preached, so they can hear
God's greatest desire is for all of creation to be brought near

That's why He gives you money to pay the cost
To take salvation and forgiveness to those who are lost
Sinners live their lives in bondage and fear of death
They know there's a hell, God hardwired it into their system

Don't listen to the new age gurus
To Mohammed, Confucius, or Buddha
Every human being knows there is a hell
Like he knows love or hunger or takes a breath

Your body breathes without you telling it
Your heart beats without you compelling it
It is the mind that says there is no God
Satan rules in that arena, until you push him out

Salvation isn't about knowing that God exists
It's about accepting His way, for everyone who enlists
Submission to Jesus is painless, a magnificent gift awaits
Righteousness in Christ comes the moment you are saved

You are made free to talk to God and to worship Him
To love Jesus and to fellowship with Him
To receive your healing and walk in blessings
To love others as God loves you, without conditions

To expect Jesus to fulfill all the promises in His word
Those are not empty words in that Book, but records
Those words are life and life more abundantly
Those words are God's promise, those words are liberty

Foundation Layer

Inspiration: This was written for a teacher and friend on the occasion of her birthday.

> *Scripture:* 1 Corinthians 12:28 (NKJV) says, "And God has appointed these in the church: first apostles, second prophets, third teachers, after that miracles, then gifts of healings, helps, administrations, varieties of tongues."

Steadfast, immovable, and sure-footed
Planted on a foundation that's deeply rooted
Stand fast in righteousness, and others will follow
Sweet lips of encouragement never echo hollow

The blasting fiery furnace does not frighten you
Don't count fear among you, Jesus walks with you
Sing for God, sing first and then a word of ministry
Obedience opens the door of the anointing

And you are anointed, a price you willingly pay
Rising early to spend time with God each day
Consistency has merit, it's faithfulness He craves
Time is a continuum that extends beyond the grave

Your husband is a man after God's heart, you follow him
Your influence grounds, nurtures, and inspires him
And the two shall become one, complete in God's image
Together nothing can stop you, run the race to the finish

Your children are many, their mouths open for the worm
They trust you to teach them to fly, thousands of little birds
Soaring to catch the wave, watch them grow and leave the nest
They make room for others, you serve them only your best

A beacon of light shines brightest in darkness
Spread your wings wide and soar over the earthly mess
The anointing flows when God's word goes forth
Love is longsuffering, it's the key to open every door

Prosperity is all-encompassing, it's who Jesus is, and what He does
Giving opens the windows of heaven, and then the blessing comes
Call them as you see them and don't be tempted to hold back
The end is coming soon, so there is a need to jerk out the slack

Everything your hand touches God prospers, He brings it to pass
Anything you want from God, just open your mouth and ask
Faith is a spirit, a spiritual force, and it receives His grace
Push out the borders, let it rip, reach out to touch God's face

The foundation layer, the cornerstone, is firm when set
Causes all the building blocks to line up straight and perfect
Your place in God is firmly established and will always be
Your time in His presence transforms you from glory to glory

Song of Joy

Inspiration: This poem is about believers entering heaven.

> *Scripture:* Revelation 4:2 (NKJV) says, "Immediately I was in the Spirit; and behold, a throne set in heaven, and *One* sat on the throne."

Sometimes taking is easier than giving
Sometimes dying is easier than living
Sometimes it comes, and sometimes it goes
Where it stops, nobody knows
Some things are hard to understand
Incomprehensible to any man

The mysteries are solved, and the darkness disappears
Resolution is of the light and assuages all fears
Can't move left or right, so go down the center
Knock three times, and careful how you enter
Entrance is free, there is no charge
God opens the door and wraps you in His arms

His arms are broad, He spreads the heavens
He receives His children who've made confessions
Jesus is Lord, Jesus who sought and saved
In the Book of the Lamb, He sees your name
Welcome, have a seat, and the song begins
The song of joy is how God receives His children

You'll miss them, it's true, but its time had come
Death is all around us outside God's kingdom
His kingdom is light, love, peace, and joy
Throw off the bands and the burdens and just enjoy
The mountains move, and from here you get to watch 'em
The rainbows flow from here, and God doesn't botch 'em

You see the light and come to the light
In the land where there is only daytime, never any night
Praise the Lord, jump up and down, and rejoice
In the land where you'll never strain to hear God's voice
Comfort and peace, I AM I AM
Released from the body, the spirit of man

About the Author

Jamie L. Cronin was called by God to serve as a missionary in Windhoek, Namibia. She served for eight years, teaching Bible studies in Katutura and volunteering at a local church. Jamie now resides in Sioux Center, Iowa. With Arms Open Wide is her first book of poems.

Printed in the United States
By Bookmasters